Since his earliest years, Nic was drawn to a sense of service to others. This was reflected in his early professional pursuits as a Personal Trainer, a CrossFit Coach, and a Youth Mentor for different organisations. His ultimate dream of serving his community was finally realised in 2017, when Nic was accepted into the South Australia Police. The next three years, as you're about to read, were a life-changing roller coaster. After being inspired by his Police service, today Nic is pursuing a career in Psychology and Wellbeing Support, while always devoting time to acting, CrossFit and Martial Arts.

First and foremost, this book is dedicated to my soulmate and the love of my life, who's a gift to this world. She shines an inspiring, selfless and pure light on anyone blessed to meet her. My path has only become clearer with her glow guiding my way and the limitless connection we share. Your belief in me inspires me every day. I love you, Erin.

To my family, who, despite me always walking on my own, often-unconventional path, have always sustained an unwavering sense of love, support and belief in me.

To my coursemates at the South Australia Police Academy, my instructors, my Field Tutors, my Sergeants, my team members, any Officer I ever worked alongside, and to every man and woman in blue upholding their sworn oath to their community day and night. This is my tribute, my celebration to the courage and service you live by every day.

Nicholas Betts

CROSSING BLUE BRIDGES

AUSTIN MACAULEY PUBLISHERS

LONDON * CAMBRIDGE * NEW YORK * SHARJAH

A CIP catalogue record for this title is available from the British Library.

ISBN 9781398491687 (Paperback)
ISBN 9781398491700 (ePub e-book)
ISBN 9781398491694 (Audiobook)

www.austinmacauley.co.uk

First Published 2024
Austin Macauley Publishers Ltd®
1 Canada Square
Canary Wharf
London
E14 5AA

I would like to acknowledge Austin Macauley Publishers for resonating with my story, seeing value in its meaning and supporting me in sharing it with an audience. You have helped me realise a dream that for over a year, while sitting on the couch writing furiously, was always a distant what-if.

This story was inspired by everyone who ever shared a single step with me throughout the following journey. To my family and friends, who supported me and saw me try and fail and try and fail again to be selected into the South Australia Police years before I was ever successful. Their ongoing encouragement and belief in my desire to achieve this dream was always a humble reminder that our different paths we choose in life are never walked alone.

To every mentor, instructor, and senior officer that I encountered from the first day I entered the gates of the Academy. At the time, my lack of knowledge was only matched by my abundance of motivation and enthusiasm. You all served as a source of inspiration through your presence, experience and investment into myself, and my fellow cadets to ensure we could stand strong and proud on a foundation of training, conduct and tradition laid by you. You ensured this foundation would be solid enough that we could feel confident after 12 of the most relentless months of my life, to leap into a new, challenging, rewarding and ultimately life-changing career. You were entrusted with the strength, service, and sacrifice that you, and so many officers before you had sworn to uphold, and to instil those same values and dedication into the next generation of officers…You walked everyday with the tradition of SAPOL on your shoulders, and through education, expectation, discipline, pressure, support and a belief in our commitment, with some blood and sweat along the way, you made us feel and love the weight of that tradition that we prepared to carry.

To every member of every team I served on, especially my field tutors…your commitment to me and my development and growth into the officer you envisioned I could be, this left me in awe and humbled every shift. You were not only outstanding operators with a wealth acquired through years of knowledge, experience, and service in the most challenging career I could ever imagine. But you took it upon yourself to carry the burden of responsibility to mentor and guide eager and hungry probationary constables, who in my case, for a long time really had no idea what the fuck we were doing. My complete lack of knowledge was only disguised by my faith in my courage and enthusiasm to face any situation and any perceived dangers with unquestionable commitment. When I was suddenly thrust from the safety and controlled environment at the Academy into the chaos and unpredictable real world with the responsibility we now carried as police officers, the consequences we faced, and the very real and present dangers suddenly were in our face every day. I feel like I didn't express this enough with all of you, but there were times I was truly humbled by your abilities to face the demands of the duty with so much self-assurance and confidence, managing the relentless workload, and all the while keeping me warm under your wing, guiding me and supporting me. I will always remember the times when you would drop whatever you were in the middle of and assist me, listen to my questions, explain something until I understood it, or take it upon yourself to share my workload even if this meant hours of time spent on my tasks, knowing how much of your own work was waiting. You were all always patient and obliging, and would put my performance, understanding and development selflessly ahead of you. Whether you still take the time to truly reflect and appreciate just what this privileged position you're in means, but I recognised the very unique and special minds that it takes to not only consistently perform the duties of a police officer with selfless devotion, but at the same time, to mentor, educate, guide and inspire someone at the beginning of their policing career. I saw all of you as role-models, graciously taking on that responsibility amidst the daily chaos that policing is.

Upon reflection now, I am truly grateful for being able to walk some of my path with you. Through some of the intense and violent situations we shared together, facing others' emotional trauma, the tough love you enacted on me simply through your passion and belief in the standard of service expected, or simply being present together in an emotionally charged or sombre moment that few people will ever even encounter once in their life. It's reflecting on these many moments that I feel a resounding sense of gratitude that I have been able to exist through so much life experience with professionals, and people serving to the highest calibre.

Finally, to every police officer and emergency services member out there. Two years of my life were spent serving the community as a police officer. Every shift, I was reminded in one way or another just how taxing, fulfilling, challenging, exciting, dangerous, terrifying, exhilarating and rewarding this service really is. In every colleague I worked with, whether we were patrol partners, team members, or crossing by one another in the hallways, I always sensed something deep inside them. Even through the many diverse personalities, the more immersed in the job I became, the more I realised the level and depth of service and commitment that each and every one of you must live by every day. This is not a career that one gets into who's only motivated by job safety and security. A steady and comfortable pay check and a predictable Monday to Friday, nine-to-five working week with a free weekend to always look forward too. Police have to be driven by something else, something more and greater beyond them self. There is nothing about this service that is safe and predictable, apart from the knowing that no matter what you may encounter that shift when you're kitting up that you will never face it alone, and you will always have your brothers and sisters in blue by your side ready at the drop of a hat to run through fire with you. There is so much in this service that most civilised members of society can never understand. There is so much in this service that has the capacity to unhinge the human mind, and officers face these monsters every day and night because that is what they have sworn to uphold and protect their community from.

I wish I could sit down with each and every one of you, and just listen to what your own individual motivations and desires to serve were. If you ask a person who has climbed, or attempted to climb Mount Everest, I doubt you would get as simple a response as, "I maxed out the incline on my gym's treadmill and wanted to get a more intense quad burn." To pursue a challenge as physically and emotionally exhausting as that, where the risk of death or injury is so high, a desire like that can only come from a place deep within a person, far beyond the rationale and understanding of others who do not share their passion or dream. But what I do know, and most in this world will always admire with awe and inspiration, is you are our real-life superheroes. You are our comic book heroes come too life, whose daily consistent commitment is hard for most people to comprehend yet is an insight into the greatness we all possess within us. You are our leaders in the community, and you personify the very best in who we are, because you are willing to confront and fight against the very worst in us.

During my time in uniform, there were so many faces and characters I can remember. No matter who you were as an individual, and no matter what connection I thought I had with you, I knew you in the blue uniform, and for this reason, of everyone I ever met, I only knew heroes.

Chapter One

"The only thing necessary for evil to conquer, is for good people to do nothing."

I had already lived through this moment maybe a few hundred times before it actually happened. When it actually did, it was so familiar too me, as if I could predict the next action to come seconds before it happened; where I was when the phone rang, the words 'Private Number' appearing on my phone screen, even what time of day it was and what I was doing. All of this was unfolding second by second, exactly how I had imagined it. As if the words I was hearing through the phone I had scripted myself and was just hearing someone else say them aloud to me. I could hear in my own voice that I was so certain in receiving this news; while in the same breath realising this wasn't another rehearsal in my mind that this was reality and that in this very moment, a dream I had envisioned so clearly in my mind and held so close to my heart, for years and years, was actually coming true.

This was the morning I received the phone call to congratulate me on being successfully selected into the South Australia Police (SAPOL). This is a moment that stands out so clearly in my mind that best represents the power of visualisation. The ability to envision and rehearse something so clearly in amongst our own thoughts, imagining every meticulous detail, from the rate of our breathing, the touch of a surface, the flood of euphoria at the sight of something and the physical sensations we'll feel from it. To be able to visualise something so clearly, that is so important to us, that eventually it finds its way from our thoughts into our reality. As if the strength, clarity, and consistency of our own thoughts has somehow crafted the physical environment around us and manifested the very experience we want right in front of us.

At the time, I was living and working in Perth. When I had progressed through the stages of selection for SAPOL, at the same time I had also progressed through the selection process for the Australian Border Force (ABF). A position in Perth was available, and I was selected to attend their next training course at their Academy. While at the time, my priority was SAPOL, and I was convinced I would be selected for it, especially after successfully progressing through all the stages of selection. In my mind, it was just a matter of time. However, I was aware of the reality that even successful completion of selection did not guarantee you would even be selected. Your name would be thrown in a pool of other candidates and depending on your overall score from all your selection phases; this would determine if you were selected for a position on an upcoming cadet course at the Academy. So yeah, you could imagine how much visualising and self-belief it would take to believe in this dream, even against the odds and when being selected could come down to a few numbers, over so many stages and against so many worthy candidates.

When the position was offered to me in Perth with ABF, I quickly accepted it but in the back of my mind, I knew that I would be ready on a day's notice to pack my bags and return to Adelaide. I was just one phone call away.

I had already been in Perth for almost three months. I had probably called SAPOL Recruiting three times to get any update, but all they could tell me was my name was in the candidates' pool, and numbers had to be organised for cadet courses before successful applicants would be contacted. In my naturally optimistic way, I took this to mean I was successful, and they were just organising themselves before telling me; it was just a matter of waiting, but not knowing for how long.

That morning, I was in my bedroom at the share house I had been living for the past few weeks. I was getting ready for a training course I had at the airport, so that's where my mind and attention was. I was putting on my uniform when my mobile began to ring and vibrate. I reached over for it on the bed, picked it up and paused when I saw 'Private Number' on the screen. Those few seconds of pause felt like hours. I held my breath, I felt my chest rise as that lump of anticipation and possibility rose in my throat, and like a sprinter, braced before the starting gun; I held the phone to my ear and spoke, "Hello, Nicholas speaking."

I'm pretty sure with the potent mix of excitement, anticipation, disbelief and that surreal sensation of this is actually happening ready to pour out of me, the person on the other end would have heard the quivering tone in my voice. I can't remember his exact words, but I do remember the warm flow of endorphins flood through me like a bucket of warm water had been steadily poured out from inside me, and I could feel it flowing through and filling up every inch of my body (I'm speaking figuratively of course, so in case you're already starting to wonder…no, I did not actually piss my pants in excitement). He said congratulations on being successful through the entire selection process, that my name had been selected from the pool of candidates, and that I would be commencing at the South Australia Police Academy on the 16th of November 2017.

What I remember so clearly throughout this moment, and the rest of that day was a heightened sense of awareness and presence. It was a surreal sensation, going to the airport that day for my training course and telling a handful of my course mates who were aware of my pursuit in making it into SAPOL, especially Pete. He had been my roommate for a month in Sydney when we did our ABF Induction and course commencement. Rooming up with someone forges a unique and open connection as you are sharing the daily occurrences with that person, and you can debrief and vent each night after the working day is finished. We would laugh about our bromance as each morning before we left for the train to get into work; he would have a cup of coffee ready for both of us. Often, the morning would start with me coming out of my room, freshly towelled after a shower, and he'd be in the kitchen to greet me with a fresh brew ready…bless that man!

I remember, early in our friendship, I shared with him my belief that Border Force was just a steppingstone until I got the call from SAPOL. I would speak to him about this with such resolve and humble belief and certainty that it would happen, you might think it had already happened. The day it did, and I told him, he recalled these conversations we'd had months ago and how my sheer belief in this vision and my calling had manifested it into my conscious reality.

The next day, I informed my course instructors, who were very understanding, supportive and encouraging and I commenced the resignation process from the Australian Border Force. I remained in Perth for another week, just soaking up the free time and letting the realisation and excitement of what had just occurred and what I was about to commence wash over me.

A few moments that stand out in my mind, and even today remain as clear and vivid as if they had happened yesterday, was saying goodbye to a friend I'd made in Perth, Emily. We had met at a training session, and quickly a close and special friendship was forged between us. One that still stands today and is characterised by an openness to share anything with each other, knowing there is so much trust, respect, and gratitude between us.

The other moments included the flight back to Adelaide, being picked up by my sister and returning home. The elation I felt on the flight home was one I had already rehearsed in my mind over and over. It would be imagining and visualising these seemingly insignificant moments and actions that would be such a powerful means of keeping me grounded and focused on the outcome I had intended. Especially through testing times and when the burden of fantasising about a dream begins to overwhelm the possibility of realising it and opens you up to doubts and realities of 'this may not even happen' and 'are you believing in a dream that just isn't real'. These self-doubts, I believe are like shadows; they are always attached to your idea, your vision, and your dream. They go wherever you go, and they're always lurking close by to any positive insights and self-belief you might have along your journey. However, that is why it was so important to me to take time to visualise some of those inevitable steps along the way to realising a dream. To me, those few minutes of closing my eyes, and playing out those small, easily forgotten moments such as receiving the phone call, or sitting on the plane destined for Adelaide with the wave of relief that my dream had come true, these actions of mentally rehearsing and visualising these inevitable moments were my greatest counter strategies to those shadows of self-doubt. What I found was the moments those shadows began to overshadow my clarity and optimistic belief, caused them to become distorted, faded and blurred in the shadowy darkness. By visualising and playing out in my mind the smallest, seemingly insignificant details and moments, it was like shining a light, instantly dissolving away their darkness and allowing me to see clearly again, with resolve and clarity, the dream I had in front of me.

We are all destined for greatness; the scale of the greatness we strive for is only defined by the detail in which we can see the path to get there.

Chapter Two

"Thursday, 16th November 2017 – First Day"

It was here, it was time. It was Thursday, the 16th of November 2017, and I was putting on my best suit and tie for my first day at the South Australia Police Academy. At the time, I was living with my parents in Woodcroft. The Academy was in Taperoo; basically the drive was from one side of South Australia to the other. However, I always enjoyed travelling and I had always done it. Whether it was for study, or to get to training, I would never hesitate or have a second thought about driving from Woodcroft to the city, between 25–50 minutes depending on the time of day for a CrossFit or martial arts class. When you're passionate about something, and I mean something that when you're not doing it, it's consuming your thoughts. Regardless of whatever other commitments you have on that day, without some time dedicated to that passion, your day is just not done. So, an extended drive to and from a destination that you know excites you, ignites that passionate flame of feeling alive. Plus, a coffee along the way just to compliment the trip and allow you some uninterrupted time alone with your thoughts, that was always an experience I thoroughly enjoyed and the 40- to 50-minute drive to the Academy would be a Monday to Friday routine for me over the next twelve months.

However, on this day, it felt more real than any of those other trips. I remember, the entire drive I was pulsing with anticipation and waves of euphoric realisation crashing over me with so much excitement that I could have rocket fuel through my veins and launch me right out of the top of my car. This was it; I was driving towards my destiny, my calling, and my dream. I drove through the staff entrance of the Academy and parked in the big open patch of grass and dirt. I began walking towards a well-manicured grassed area and a long stretch of stairs leading into a large building. The grassed area was the official Parade Ground, where graduating courses would march out on their final day.

When I had entered the carpark, there was a person standing at the entrance, dressed in police uniform, with the traditional peak cap, and a blue band around the base of the cap. Plus, two blue bands on their shoulders, with the word 'cadet' written in white. These blue bands would be the identifying insignia of a police cadet still in training. The moment you could remove these bands was a profound and powerful moment of achievement that I was a long 12 months away from being realised.

This cadet directed me into the carpark. Another cadet, standing near the stairs on the Parade Ground, welcomed me and directed me inside the building. I entered what appeared to be an assembly hall, with rows of chairs set up, large flags and commemorating plaques and boards signifying a place of history and tradition. You can imagine that SAPOL is rich in both. The first few rows were full of other people dressed in casual corporate attire. I smiled as I saw the tense and nervous expressions of anticipation and expectation all over their faces.

This would be my course, my family over the next 12 months. I would see these people every Monday to Friday (and some weekends) over the next year. I would share every experience of our training with them as SAPOL ensured we were already to their standard and expectations as they laid down a solid foundation for us to commence our careers as police officers but in this moment, it was like the first day of kindergarten for adults.

I sat next to another guy and quickly introduced myself. His name was Ryan. Over the coming months, he and I would become good friends. He was many years younger, but he had a sense of laid-back maturity and unassuming self-assurance that would see him successful. The best way I can describe the first impression he must have had of me was an overly friendly Saint Bernard that has just consumed an excess amount of sugar. My excitement to be there, to be connecting with others who were sharing this moment of being at the beginning of one of the most exciting adventures we would face, well yeah…my excitement couldn't be contained.

The cadets I had seen upon entering the carpark turned out to be course members of a course that had started only a short time before us. This was one of many traditions for the junior course to welcome the next course on their first day. They spoke to us and shared as much as they could in the time they had, about the wild, chaotic, fast-paced and pressure filled world we had now just become a part of.

We were led to our classroom, our learning hub for the next twelve months and sat in pairs. The person you were paired with would be your patrol partner for the next phase of training, and the person you would complete all your scenarios and practical with. Then entered our course mentors, two sergeants, one of whom would be with us until graduation. Some people exude a presence about them the moment they enter a room. To me, this sergeant exuded the very essence and presence of a police officer, and no surprise, after accumulating over 30 years in the job. He appeared physically fit, with sculpted arms for a man his age (sorry Sarge! Age is just a number). He was a gifted storyteller and we would enjoy many moments over the coming months where he would regale us with 'waries' from his career. He had the gift of the gab and a cheeky quick wit but also carried with him the respect and assurance of years of experience as an officer, and you got a sense that he was someone whose respect you wanted to earn, that you never wanted to disappoint him, let alone ever cross him. To me, he personified the standard of personal and professional excellence this career could allow you to attain.

Over the next couple of days, our time at the Academy was full of introductions; to staff, to different areas of the Academy that we would spend countless hours, like the Parade Ground, the scenario village, the computer labs, and the library (many hours spent here). In fact, before I commenced at the Academy, a friend of mine already in the police described what the academic Academy experience would be like. I was a university student at the time. He goes, "The Academy is actually a similar study load to university, except the equivalent to a high distinction at university is only a pass mark on an Academy exam, and you basically just have to memorise everything word for word. It's a lot more fast-paced and a tonne more pressure." Given my university experience already, being a full-time student and as much as I enjoyed spending a lot of late nights at the university library (seriously, I used to love going in at the end of the day with a coffee and motivational music and just immersing in my work with no time constraints). So, the thought of the Academy being comparable to a full-time academia institute, I laughed casually when he told me this. I couldn't understand why he didn't and remained stoic and bare faced looking back at me. In a few months, I would understand why."

My fellow course mates and I would stand and watch the senior courses conduct their morning parade which is basically a series of marching formations, and the morning rollcall is taken. These first few mornings you really feel like the little duck in the big pond of seniors. All the courses are in uniform, in formation and moving as one. We are standing there, a disorganised unexperienced mess in our 'civil' corporate wear. The rest of the time we would take care of all the paperwork and admin required when commencing with a new organisation.

Sometime during our first week, we had our first session with our Operational Safety Training staff, affectionately known as OST. These were the senior instructors responsible for our physical training, practical scenarios, self-defence and qualifying us in all our tactical options. Many course members would come to dread these sessions, whether it was their general dislike for physical exercise, the military-style degree of discipline and urgency the staff enforced on us, or the pressure and excitement of the role-plays and practical assessments. But many of my other course mates and I loved these sessions. They would recreate and remind us of the very real intensity and exertion that would be demanded of us on duty.

I love fitness; I've been doing it for so long now that it's more of a psychological experience and therapeutic release. The physical benefits are simply a daily reminder of how proud you should feel within yourself, knowing the hard work and commitment you prove to yourself to forge that physical capability. Anyone who exudes a sense of purity, self-awareness, humility, and self-assurance understands the importance of physical health and fitness. Especially the ability to push to an intensity in a workout when every sense and instinct inside you is screaming at you to stop or rest a few seconds longer. We were reminded regularly at the Academy of how essential physical performance is for police, and there would be many times in my years of serving ahead, where my physical ability determined the outcome of a situation. The famous belief that the mind will give up long before the body ever will, that is never any more true than when you're in the middle of a violent confrontation, or chasing a suspect on foot, and I firmly believe that anyone who doesn't take their physical conditioning seriously in this career is doing themselves, and their colleagues a serious injustice, and even putting them at serious risk. Whether you like fitness or not, you've entered a career where your physical conditioning can be the singular defining factor between you, your colleagues, or an innocent party being seriously injured…or worse. This was a huge source of excitement for me joining this career, as I always have had a healthy, sometimes unhealthy obsession with fitness and training, I felt like there would be no better career for me than one that demands a sustained level of fitness to get the job done successfully, and where your physical capabilities could be a huge factor in forging your reputation amongst your peers.

As I would come to appreciate on a much deeper level on probation, physical fitness and maintaining a consistent workout regime served even more as a mental stabiliser, a way to fuel any tensions and stress built up during shifts and express them in a healthy wave of intensity and frenzied exercise, where the only limitations as to how much were entirely on me. This had an empowering effect of reprioritising the degree of stress I was placing on different things. By giving me humble reassurance that I could exert myself physically and mentally by striving beyond my pre-conceived barriers and even more important, loving this challenge and experience. When you feel empowered with that sense of confidence, there is nothing anyone or anything can ever say or do to try intimidate you. Because with an unassuming resolve, they have no idea that you can and will shake the Earth if you choose too, you train every day to remind yourself of that belief. Fitness is the heat, the iron in the fire that forges the strength of our steel, our souls and sharpens our greatest asset, the mind.

This was an easy source of motivation for me when doing PT sessions or practical scenarios in front of the OST instructors, all of the senior members are experienced police officers who know exactly how real the threat is on the streets. When you have experienced police officers watching over you and observing the level of your mental toughness and fortitude, in my mind there is no option, and I will happily push until my heart explodes or physically my body starts to break down (even if my arms fall off, I can still squat!). It's a deep insight into a person's character, how they manage themselves through physical distress and discomfort. It's an even greater one, how they respond to failure.

This was no more apparent than when the day came that we would all enjoy the full experience of getting OC sprayed, one of our tactical options. It was very effective in causing immediate discomfort, disorientation, and usually aggravation, which when dealing with a non-compliant suspect, these feelings would then usually lead to compliance. It is important for all officers to understand the sensation of spray. It can happen when arriving at a job as back up, that if spray has been deployed, you could run straight into it, and being familiar with the effects is already a huge advantage to working through it and still getting the job done.

We were getting sprayed at the end of this day. Whatever classes or lectures we had throughout that day were probably insurmountable…everyone's minds were on that last session, and you could feel the tension and nervousness building as the moment drew closer. Finally, we got changed into our OST gear. This was a pair of blue trousers, separate to our uniform so we could sweat and get scuffed up in, and a plain dark blue shirt. We got into formation, marching in pairs, and were led down to the scenario village. Next to a two-storey scenario house was a small square tin shed, which we were informed during our first weeks was the spray shed. Basically, the shed would be filled with spray with us in it. We were informed that we would be the first course to trial a different, more scenario-based spray experience. One that simulated closely a situation that we could find ourselves in and required us to execute trained tactical procedures while affected by spray.

The scenario was as follows, sprint about 200 metres around the park area in the middle of the village, about two laps, do five burpees, and then sprint into the shed. Once inside, they kept you in there for a short time, asking you questions such as what's your ID number, and spell your course mentor's name in the phonetic alphabet. Once you're good and 'spiced' up, run out of the shed and approach a 'suspect' who you then have to give verbal commands as we'd been instructed on before. These involved getting them to turn around, hands interlocked behind their head, and then execute the correct procedure to apply handcuffs. All the while, fighting through the effects of the OC spray to ensure that you can still operate under distress.

There were a couple times I can remember arriving at a scene, where officers were already in attendance. You could tell instantly that spray had been deployed, usually by the ominous exaggerated blinking of officers and suspects, usually the suspect is obvious about the effects as they rant and rave, plus the crinkling up of the nose, and rapid shaking of the head like a dog that's just been stung by a bee on the nose.

I put my hand straight up when they asked who wanted to do the scenario first. I couldn't wait to get sprayed. I have always had a burning fascination with the extremes in life, whether it's something like this that commonly has a fear-inducing reaction in people, or a physical challenge that is usually deemed 'stupid' or simply disgusting by others perception of it. Physical and mental anguish to these capacities have always naturally drawn me in rather than push me away. The only way I can describe it is a motivation to squeeze every opportunity out of life without one ounce of regret or unfulfillment. So, when something comes up that is confronting enough to usually repel most away, I'm usually compelled to jump in and try it. Perhaps now, being a few years older and wiser, I may consider things with a little more contemplation and patience rather than the type of dog-tongue-flapping-out-the-window type of impulsive recklessness I used to run into things with.

This was the reason I nearly broke my neck in early high school on a school camp, jumping from the top of a sand dune and rag-dolling all the way to the bottom (I wish I had kept the footage from this though; the reaction of those around me when I jumped from the top ledge, landed on my neck and got spat out tumbling down the dune is worth the watch). It's also the reason I broke my ankle in Year 10, when I jumped off a roof in a mate's backyard. I was actually sober and jumped off the roof so I could get down faster as they were just bringing out the beers. This side of me that was always an underlying driving force saw me fall in love with training, fitness and specifically CrossFit and martial arts, and to compete in CrossFit, which is itself, a descent into one's own odyssey of self-inflicted pain-inducing intensity and exhaustion. It's always been present when I've participated in events like Tough Mudder or why I enlisted in the Army Reserves (during my basic training at Kapooka. On one particular day, when we were traversing an obstacle course, I got berated by the drill instructors for jumping free-fall from a tower and only applying the brakes on my safety harness at the last second). It is this draw to the extreme and surreal that I always firmly believed a career as a police officer would satisfy and fulfil these cravings.

I took my place at the front of the line, and on the call of the instructor, took off sprinting my way around the scenario village twice, before banging out my burpees and charging full throttle into the shed. Once I was in there, I quickly became aware of the misty cloud of spicy dust that had filled the room. I turned and was looking out the window to the instructor who was observing me, and he began to ask me questions or give me instructions: spell your name in the phonetic alphabet. Who is your course mentor? No, spell their name in the phonetic alphabet! As I was trying to get my words out, I could notice a slight burning, irritable sensation in my throat, and over my skin. It was nothing more than if I had just eaten some spicy curry, and coughing as a reaction to the heat, or a sensation on my skin like sunburn. Eventually, they released me. I came charging out of the shed, confident and feeling unstoppable as I wasn't feeling much impact from the spray. I ran up to one of my course mates who was role playing an offender, and I gave him the verbal commands we had been taught to get him to comply and in a position that I could put handcuffs on him behind his back. My words came out unaffected, and I wasn't showing any effects from the spray whatsoever. I'll admit, it was a pretty badass moment in my mind, to be unphased and unaffected in the eyes of our instructors and my fellow course mates. Then one by one, they all had their turn. Because I was the first one in the shed, perhaps there was some speculation that the density of the spray cloud hadn't reached its full thickness in the shed, but I didn't want to discredit what I had just done. Some of the sights of seeing my course mates running out of the shed, spluttering, and crying was, well, just a little amusing. Sure enough, our course mentors were standing by with a camera to capture these special moments for memorabilia when our course graduated. I remember my sergeant taking one photo of me with my mate. He had just had his turn and I had my arm around him with a big open grin on my face, and he looked like his head was melting off his shoulders. I wish I had gotten that photo. I was hovering around where people would run out of the shed to confront the offender, to show my encouragement. One of my mates, who got really affected, came staggering out of the shed, crunched over and his head lowered to the ground. To emphasise the urgency in getting to the offender, and to push through the effects of the spray, knowing we couldn't let that affect our performance of our duties, a couple of the instructors got around him and offered him some of their well-intended encouragement and support. As they were yelling at him and directing him to keep moving, by now they were close to him bearing down on him, he has reared his head up and sent a trail of snot and tears spraying into the air. "Oh shit!" one of the instructors had yelled mid-sentence, and as they quickly jumped back and gave him a few feet of room as he spluttered, cried and spat his way through the rest of the exercise.

Chapter Three

"There's nothing like being pushed with your back up against the wall to remind you that the only direction you can go is forward."

Phase Three: this signified the top of the mountain for our Academy journey. After this, it was all downhill, just another 'Out Phase' (time away from the Academy, like work experience spending time on the job and working alongside real officers), driver training (intense, but I'll get into that later) and Phase Five (the final phase before graduation). I had been told from friends who were weeks or months ahead at the Academy than me, that the final few weeks of Phase Three signified the most stressful, and pressure-filled time of the year. The workload would suddenly be so insurmountable, that you couldn't believe where all the paperwork had come from so suddenly. This included, mandatory paperwork for numerous practical scenarios, and studying and preparing for the end-of-phase-three exam, which was an accumulation of all the knowledge and legislation we as a course had been taught from the beginning of the course, until now. Basically, I understood what my mate had previously told me about the workload comparing to university. We were at the Academy Monday to Friday, from about 8:00 a.m. until about 5:00 p.m., and then I quickly realised I could easily be spending another couple hours or more on campus, either training, studying in the library or a combination of both.

While I noticed the workload increased, from a few seemingly cruisy first few weeks at the beginning of the phase, to suddenly having a mammoth mountain of assessments to submit, resubmit or study and prepare for. I took this as a personal challenge to further excel in my capabilities and performance. I was living a career I had dreamt of and believed in for so long. This was everything I had spent so many hours visualising and fantasising about, imagining how I would feel in these very moments if it was to ever come true, and how grateful and appreciative I would be just to be given the opportunity to live my dream. Reflecting on this, there was never any amount of work or expectation that could weaken the strength I had from my gratitude to be there. Being a dream of mine for so long, that just the very thought of being immersed in this career would excite me, I would happily grind away for weeks and months with no sleep if that's what it took, and if that was even physically possible. Working nightshifts would actually take me as close to this reality of sleepless days I had ever experienced so far in life. But we'll get into that later.

A trait of mine that I am very proud of, and very clear about is the degree of optimism and positivity that I naturally possess. Anyone who knows me well enough, or who is even getting to know me would probably agree, I am always consistently positive and optimistic, no matter what is happening in my life or what the subject of conversation is. It's always interesting to me how this quality can be misinterpreted depending on the outlook of the person looking at me. I have told people who I have quickly realised in their interactions with me, or my interpretation to their response to something I say, "Don't confuse kindness or positivity with weakness." Or even for people who have identified my consistent positive nature as something unnatural or unrealistic, perhaps associating with some degree of ignorance or being naive. My own understanding of this perception is they perceive this as lacking in other qualities. How can you think positively about anything that most people would look at with defeat, disappointment, sad emotions or even trauma? My thinking to that sort of opinion, is my depth of self-awareness, my emotional intelligence, clarity, and self-reflection. Yes, I can recognise how something, or someone has had an effect that can upset another or cause sadness, or anger or frustration. However, I choose to seek out the light in these darkest moments. Be aware of the darkness you're in, but intentionally seek the light. The light will shine its brightest when it is surrounded by darkness. However, you have to be actively seeking it, especially when you are surrounded and consumed by darkness, when positive emotions or strength seem the furthest away and even impossible given the present circumstance. This would be a quality I would recognise in others throughout my time as a probationary constable. One situation was the appreciation and thankfulness a grieving son shared with me, while his father lay deceased only a few metres away. I was one of the first responding officers to this situation. The paramedics were still working on the father, and his two sons and other family members were present, holding their breath that their father would survive. I was with the son throughout this and recognising the full gravity and trauma of the situation, I was as patient, respectful, and empathetic as I could be for a son whose losing his father. Just moments after my responsibilities at the scene were finished, and I shared my condolences with him and other family. Despite him obviously being consumed with grief and loss, the son found the strength within himself to acknowledge me and share his appreciation and gratitude for my presence and comfort through that time. No matter how dark, or seemingly disastrous a situation may seem, where it feels like all hope is lost, a person with emotional intelligence, clarity within their own thoughts and awareness of their ever-changing present state (or even just an appreciation for this) can always remain grounded and navigate the chaos around them. They can seek out the strength they gain from this situation or something they can take from it that can benefit their self-development. Whether that strength and grounding is for themselves or others around them, like having the will, awareness, and strength in a dire moment to recognise and express gratitude for the presence of another.

So this brings me back to spending late nights in the Academy library, studying, and completing paperwork. I am also very routine orientated, and once I have that routine in place, few things will ever shake me from it or deter my consistency. In this case, that would mean keeping a balance between nights that I would train at the Academy gym, perhaps getting in a shorter workout than usual, and emphasising more time towards the library, or being comfortable with the decision that I would not make it to the gym tonight, because study was the priority. I kept this consistent balance right through until the end of this busy time. However, the greatest test for me came in the last week of Phase Three.

From memory, my course mates and I sat our Phase Three exam on the Monday of the last week of Phase Three. That light I was talking about earlier, well this week was maybe the first time that that light had started to flicker just bright enough to see the finish line through these last few days. I came in on Monday feeling focused and prepared. I had been studying diligently and started serious study early, knowing there was so much more content to memorise for this exam than any previous. Plus, some of the legislation this time was more wordy and lengthy, so it took a few more goes to really cement it into my head.

At the end of the exam, I felt relatively secure in how confident I was with how it went, but we didn't get results until later in the day. When that time came, I forget if the instructor read out our results or if we went up individually. What I do remember was the result…78%.

Now, if I was still at university, I would have been beaming and stoked to get back a mark like that. By university standards, that was a distinction. Unfortunately, by the Academy's standards, anything less than 80% is a fail. So, what happens now?

This was actually the beginning of one of the most impactful experiences I had that I am truly grateful for during my time at the Academy. It forced me to realise what I am really capable of when all the pressure and expectation lands on me. Even more importantly, it showed me that when I'm faced with failure, what type of mindset I can naturally adopt and what subsequent actions I can take.

But there's no denying the shot to the guts, and the cold wave of disappointment that is always felt in the sudden shock of these moments. That 2% meant I was in for probably my most stressful week at the Academy. Failing an exam meant you had one more chance to re-sit it and pass. This re-sit would take place first thing on that Thursday morning. I, and a couple of other course mates who also had to re-sit, would have to be at the Academy before 7:00 a.m. ready to go. It had to be that early, because on that same day was our end-of-phase practical scenarios assessment day. Any other time, I would be pumped for scenarios day! It was a full day of mock patrolling. You and your patrol partner would be on foot patrol throughout the Academy and would either be tasked to or come across different situations, where we had to put our training and knowledge into practice and pretend to be police officers and that we actually knew what we were doing. Real officers were invited to role-play and would graciously give up their time to play as victims or offenders. At the conclusion of each scenario, they would provide you and your partner feedback. It really was an awesome day! I'm very much a practical person, I can get restless easily and this was as close to the action as we could get, in this stage of my career it was a brief insight into what the job of policing would look and feel like. It's a day that is as much fun as it is long, as you could be dealing with anywhere from two to maybe four or five individual scenarios.

So, you can probably imagine now, the very last thing you would want to possibly do at the beginning of this day is re-sit an important exam, where a second failure might very well mean you are considered ineligible to progress and you are back-coursed. This means, you are removed from your course and put in another course that is a few weeks before you in their training, or at the beginning of the phase you are about to complete. It also means, should you

27

make it to graduation, you do not get to graduate with your original course mates, but rather the course you're back-coursed into. While there's no shame in this whatsoever, there was no way in hell that I was not marching out with the people that I had begun this journey with. So, I really felt like my back was against the wall after receiving my exam results.

This was probably one of the few times in my life that I really felt disappointed and frustrated with myself, where my usually consistent and reliable optimism felt shot for a few moments. Only because I knew that that failure had set me up for another week of hard studying, late nights at the library, and the expectation and pressure to perform at a time when all of my other course mates would be relaxing and enjoying the freedom of knowing they had succeeded through the most testing time at the Academy. Imagine walking out of your last high-school exam, ready to party and celebrate with your classmates that exams were over, and the school term was finished, only to be told you would be sitting that exam again at the end of the week…and if you didn't pass that, you might have to re-sit the entire school term again, fuck!

From that Monday until early that Thursday morning, I felt like I was in a constant state of focus and controlled frenzied motivation. We still had lectures and exercises to fill up our days, but the entire time, I felt restless and somewhat distracted, as I knew all my attention and every waking second needed to be spent on studying and memorising for the exam. I actually couldn't wait for the day to be finished, so I could get comfortable in the library, often with a coffee to enhance the experience and deeply immerse in concentrated revision without any distractions or other demands on my time. Each night leading up to that Thursday morning, I wouldn't leave the library until I was certain, with no doubt in my mind, that the material was firmly cemented deep in my psyche. I would have happily slept on the benches in the changeroom overnight, if it meant I could stay for a few more hours to prepare. It's always been interesting to me and exhilarating at the natural response to achieving a short-term goal, especially one that relied on your performance and preparation to achieve a standard. I loved this aspect of my time at university, spending late nights at the library or going in for a few hours in my own time to work on assignments or study for exams. These moments always instilled in me a great sense of purpose and achievement. One of the most satisfying sensations is knowing every second of every hour of every day is being spent fulfilling a goal, working towards it, and proving to yourself that you have that capability to set yourself a target and then methodically, diligently, and consistently work towards it. In these moments, one of the most important mindsets for me to adopt, and consistently practice was letting go of the result. Completely removing any expectation I had of succeeding or failing. If I had a goal, some of the biggest ones for me were the regular assessments and tests throughout university and pursuing selection for SAPOL, all my emphasis, effort, focus, and energy would be poured into the quality and thoroughness of my preparation. I wanted to go into these assessments with complete resolve and unquestionable faith in my knowing that there was absolutely nothing else that I could have possibly done to prepare myself to perform and express my true and full potential. Entering an interview, or an assessment, anything that is testing our knowledge or ability is actually a really enjoyable and exciting experience for me. Because I know I have come prepared, to the best of my ability and in this moment, all those countless hours, late nights, visualising and believing in myself, all that commitment I now get to express in my performance, and celebrate my hard work and showcase the essence of who I am.

I truly believe the best way to dissolve any performance anxieties is to be relentless, tenacious, even obsessive in preparing yourself for that moment while simultaneously letting go of your own expectations of the outcome. The worst feeling I can imagine going into these moments would be knowing, deep inside yourself that you are underprepared. That if you're being honest with yourself, that you could have put in more late nights or used those hours of procrastinating to actually focus and work. Even if the result is a failure (and by consistently practicing this philosophy I'm sharing with you, reflecting on it now, there really hasn't been many times I can even remember failing), I seriously would feel the same satisfaction as success. As long as your own accountability to yourself and the effort and commitment you put in up too that moment is true and honest. Failure is never to be feared when you're honestly proud of the effort to prepare, but a half-hearted approach while still expecting success is doing yourself a complete injustice. I will elaborate on this point, because I understand how that one could be hard for some people to fathom. Naturally, with success comes the elation and relief of achieving your goal and knowing all your hard work has counted for something. However, it is only our perception of what success and failure is that elicits an emotional reaction. I see success as an inevitable and even unsurprising outcome, if you are truly investing your best effort and energy to your time and consistent preparation. When you can stand at the door of the hallway, moments before they usher you in for your end of semester exam and know within yourself that there was truly nothing else within your power that you could have done to be ready for this moment that humble certainty should already be a source of pride before you have even sat down. This truth, when I reflect on it, is also the primary reason why I never feel disappointed with failure. If the result is not what I require or even expected, I am actually grateful as it's an honest account of how I prepared, and it gives me valuable feedback (even more so than succeeding). Was there any cracks in my efforts to be ready, or how honest am I being with myself about my consistent effort. So any perceived failure in life, I only see as an opportunity to learn and grow. I reflect and look deep within myself to better understand how I fell short in that moment. The answers are always there, if you're truly honest with yourself, and with that comes the actions for next time that you can implement to ensure that next time you have an even greater chance of achieving what you've set out for.

So, this brings us back to this example. Yes I had failed, but I did not feel like it was due to any lack of effort on my part. But what it did was take me to a place I have rarely felt, and that is feeling like a caged beast, angry and frustrated at myself and hungry, ready to be unleashed on my second opportunity. It's a very relentless feeling, similar to a controlled aggression where you now feel unstoppable in pursuing this goal, and any of those little cop-outs or excuses such as convincing yourself you don't need to stay late a few extra hours or being easily distracted when you know you should be concentrating. Those become non-existent, completely irrelevant as you are being fuelled by a degree of motivation and purpose that maybe cannot be felt until your back is against a wall, and you are left with no other option but to drive forward.

Having quickly come to terms with the disappointment of my result, and the initial frustration of knowing after so many hours of study, when I should be celebrating crossing the finish line, that I would have one more week of late nights, I quickly channelled my frustrations into focus and prepared myself for a frenzied attack on the library. Like I said, feeling like that caged beast, I couldn't wait for the day to finish just so I could get to the library, and immerse in concentrated focused study.

Thursday morning arrived, and I remember waking up in the same way I would feel on the morning of a CrossFit competition. I was ready, mentally, and physically primed for a long day of concentration, focus, performance, and assessment. I got to the Academy extra early as I had to re-sit the exam at 7:00

a.m. I met with my other course-mates who had to do it, and the sergeant took us into a quiet room where he would supervise us as we worked. I knew what was on the line and what potentially could happen if I missed the mark again but I had come in this morning with a quiet sense of resolve and self-assurance. Like I had mentioned earlier, I had complete faith in the effort of preparation I had put in up to this moment, especially in this past week. It's a feeling of such belief in effort, that a successful outcome is the only outcome you have room in your mind to believe. I wouldn't allow that much grind and hard work to lead towards anything else.

I remember as we commenced our few minutes of reading time, the exhilaration washed over me. As I was reading through each question, the answers, as clear as if they were on a sheet of paper next to me, were running through my mind. I don't think I made any notes during that time, all I remember was waiting for our test time to commence, knowing that not a single second could be wasted if I wanted to answer every question in the timeframe.

Once we started, it was like leaping into the river, and just letting yourself go with the current; entering that flow-state where your focus, concentration and intention all combine in perfect harmony to see you executing at your potential. Everything was automatic for me from this point, I was scribbling the answers out as hard and as fast as I could, ensuring that I included every single essential word or meaning. By the end, I felt that familiar wave of elation and excitement, feeling almost a mathematical certainty that I could not fail this time. I let that positive relief rush over me before heading out and kitting up, ready for our practical scenarios. The practical day is a long and exhausting day, even without having to sit an exam in the early morning before starting. But it was amazing to me how energised I could feel coming out of that exam, feeling like I just accomplished a goal that was heavy with pressure and expectation on me. Feeling purposeful and fulfilled has that ability to invigorate us, it ignites in us the true meaning of feeling alive. I've tried to live by my own motto for a long time now; there's a difference between living your life and feeling alive. What I've come to understand is that feeling can be inspired by moments of accomplishment, layered with a sense of pride in your belief and effort to overcome adversity. We can only ever feel the full impact and euphoria in these moments when they are born from something that has confronted us or forced us to face our uncertainty and doubts head on. By doing so, we are challenged to express our best self through our best effort, and sometimes without our back against that wall, leaving us no option but to push forward. We don't appreciate the courage and strength within us to make this decision.

To conclude this chapter, I received the news later that day that I had passed. While I hadn't left any doubt in my mind that I would succeed, you can never completely ease up until your result is confirmed. Receiving that confirmation and the warm blanket of relief that comes with it, really instilled in me a sense of pride and accomplishment, and I reflected back to the start of the week and what I had felt then, and what that feeling had triggered in me. I had shown myself, that under pressure, I can access another level of focus and performance. But doing that for a written exam was just the beginning.

Chapter Four

"Flow State"

We did it, my course mates and I had scaled the top of the mountain that was Phase Three. Now we had a well-deserved break from the Academy, and entered Phase Four, our second Out Phase and the three-week Police Driving Course. The course would be divided, and half would do driver training first, while the others completed Out Phase first. Driver training was seen as one of the milestones of a cadet's time at the Academy. There were usually two clear responses someone would give you when you would ask how they were feeling about driver training. Either they'd say how excited they were and couldn't wait to get into it…or their face might tense up slightly; they'd take a heavy sigh and tell you they just couldn't wait for it to be over.

Driver training was three weeks of progressively intensive exercises and assessments, designed to qualify a cadet with the 1A and 1B licence. The 1A licence was earnt at the end of week two. This meant you had demonstrated to your instructors that you were proficient in driving to a standard necessary on patrols, including such skills as moving through traffic, navigating, being proficient in cornering, moving through roundabouts without losing speed, back street driving, driving at about 10–20 km over 50 km in the back streets and being able to execute turns or J-turns at speed in the very last instant as your instructor called out the command. 1A is usually easy enough to obtain if you follow your instructor's guidance as they push you more each day to progress your confidence and skillsets. 1B is your Pursuit Driving Licence, and this isn't as easy to gain. However, it was during this assessment that I experienced one of the most profound feelings of flow, and what it means to exist and perform in that flow-state.

As I mentioned before, if I was one of the people you asked about how I was feeling about driver training, I would have become the bouncing happy goat and skipped circles around you trying to explain how excited I was. I'm a sucker for anything exciting, anything that raises your pulse, gets your blood pumping and adrenaline loose. I couldn't wait.

The first week was really just the instructor getting a feel for your current driving style and ability, and if there was anything really outstanding that they needed to focus on. There were three of us in the car each day, the instructor, me and another course mate. One would drive while the other sat in the back, and then swap over.

Probably the highlight of those three weeks had to be the couple of days we spent at Mallala Raceway. For anyone who was apprehensive or dreading driver training, this would have been the moment when you could politely say they've soiled themselves. Mallala was the point of the sword, the necessary skillsets and proficiency to obtain your 1B, if you could put it all together in the final assessment.

Our time at Mallala was only a couple of days, but as intense an experience as you could ever imagine. I would remind myself this is an experience people would happily pay for, and for us, this was an essential skillset in our role. Mallala was the instructors' opportunity to push us to limits we were already uncomfortable with, and then ensure we kept our foot on the gas and accelerated through them…literally! I remember the first day there, I was doing things in a car I have never done before, and as exciting as it was, it went against my very instincts of what to do when you're behind the wheel of a machine with total control for the safety of yourself and others. For example, accelerating to 80 kmph and intentionally oversteering and losing control of the vehicle, so you could train in regaining control. If that isn't the essence of contradiction.

This drill was upskilling us in the art of oversteering and understeering. There would be three of us in the car, one of us driving, the instructor in the passenger seat and most likely, a tense fellow course mate digging in their heels and clenching any secure surface they could bury their fingers into. On a straight stretch of the track, the driver would accelerate to 80 kmph, and at this speed, and only this speed they would make a sudden and sharp right turn at the command of the instructor. The car would oversteer and lose control, before a turn of the steering wheel in the opposite direction, at the right time would regain control and bring the car to a sudden stationary position. More often than not, cadets would be accelerating and then instincts would make them oversteer at a slower speed, as moving at 80 kmph is fast, and feels like 80 kmph. Instructors would not allow this, and you would go again and again until you were confident to hit that speed and execute the turn.

Being on a racetrack, it would only seem fair to be able to drive a car, and its driver to greater and testing limits. We would open the cars up on the straights, reaching in excess of 180 kmph, and once again being forced to accelerate through our natural instincts and preconceived limits, that being, approaching corners at these speeds or just under and at the very last second, entering the corner straight, washing speed off by braking on the straight, turning into the corner to maintain speed and accelerating through it. Once this is repeated enough times, like any skill you rise beyond the anxieties and uncertainties of feeling awkward or out of control, and you gather a sense of strength and ability that nurtures your self-assurance and confidence to push to new boundaries with these newfound skills.

Other drills we practiced were based around obstacles. Cones were set up at areas of the track, and they would simulate cornering quickly to evade an obstacle or sharp corners, a quick left and right. Or changing lanes around another vehicle at high speeds. We also rehearsed an overtaking drill. One which we would practice in the dead of night on open country roads. Imagine a convoy, the lead car reaches a speed of about 60 kmph and maintains this, the middle car matches this speed. Once on a straight, the rear car has a small window to accelerate up to the rear of the middle car, pull out and floor it, overtaking the lead car (which is still holding at 50/60 kmph) before entering the next bend. It was an exciting drill that required everyone doing their parts to precision, and without the rear car's driver having the belief they can make it to the front in time, which basically means putting the pedal through the floor of the car to cover ground, there was the very real potential of cutting another car off, hesitating and possibly colliding…exciting stuff! It was seriously wicked!

All these drills and practice were preparing us for the final assessment, what we would have to pass in order to gain our 1B Pursuit Licence. While it was a great accomplishment to pass the assessment and gain the 1B, it wasn't the end of the world if it didn't happen. Many officers serve without the 1B licence, and they come back to Mallala at a later time to reattempt the assessment. I was going into this test refusing to believe that that was even a possibility for me. For one, this was your best shot at getting it, as we had done nothing but drive cars for nearly three weeks, and we had practiced all the manoeuvres and drills so much that they were instinctive now. There was no more ideal time to get that 1B than right now.

The test was a pursuit scenario, I would be in a marked fleet (meaning a police car with lights and sirens) with an instructor assessing me in the passenger seat, facing the opposite way down the main straight. Another instructor would be in an unmarked fleet (the opposite to a marked fleet) sitting parallel to me facing the right way down the straight. At the commencement, the 'suspect's' car would take off, I had to activate lights and sirens and do a 180 degree turn and accelerate down the straight. At the first bend was a mock roundabout, set up with cones. I had to enter the roundabout, through a stop sign (failure to come to a complete stop at this stop sign, even for a second was an instant fail). Drive through the roundabout back onto the track and pursue the suspect. While reaching max speeds as before and negotiating corners without losing speed or control, and there were a few obstacles set up throughout the track. The first one was driving through a double bend, which simply required a sudden left turn immediately into a right turn. This was executed at such a speed, and so late that you couldn't see the cones around you; you just trusted from the timing and feeling of the car that you were through. A couple more bends, where failing to enter and exiting them as we had practiced would lose too much speed and time. On a straight was the obstacle simulating swerving around traffic, changing lanes, and then whipping back into your lane. Travelling at those speeds, it was a quick turn of the wheel at the right time that ensured efficiency. Another couple of sharp turns, all about timing and precision and then flooring it on the straight across the finish line – simple. This circuit had to be completed twice without the roundabout on the second lap, which meant you entered the first bend coming out of the straight at max speed. The angle of the bend meant that you did not need to brake at all. When we were all new to this, actions like that felt unnatural when you're travelling at such high speeds. But amazing what repetition in a short time can do, alleviating any previous uncertainties and doubts, and opening yourself up, enabling yourself to perform at your full potential.

The two laps had to be completed in under 4 minutes 20 seconds, and you were only allowed one cone to be hit. Otherwise, failing in any of these would mean you could have another attempt at it later in the day, and that's it.

Now, Flow State is a concept I was very excited to explore in these memoirs, because it was an experience that was so surreal and impactful too me that it left me stunned and with a new sense of clarity and belief long after the experience happened. My understanding of entering flow state was something I was deeply fascinated by from the first time I heard it. I first saw it on YouTube, from a group of extreme sports athletes detailing their experience of flow, and the commonality of freedom through performance that was shared amongst them. I next downloaded and listened to The Rise of Superman by Steven Kotler which explored in-depth the phenomenon of flow, different athletes achieving seemingly impossible feats, and the key factors and triggers that enabled them to reach a state of higher consciousness, heighten sensory awareness and a profound connection with one's own sense of self, in a moment where they felt they were physically performing to their absolute potential, or even beyond and yet it was occurring in the most natural and effortless way.

Upon reflection of my experience, I realised that many of the same factors that were connected to enabling a person to enter flow were present for me. To my understanding, these included the repetition and competency achieved in a particular skill, that has been enhanced through applying it in progressively more demanding scenarios, and thereby reinforcing its instinctual and habitual execution. Another was the pressure of assessment, whereby I am accountable for the level of my performance and the mental rehearsal of success and visualisation before the event actually takes place. Plus, the ever-present consequence of risk that if these skills are not executed to absolute precision and with your completely immersive present state and concentration, the consequence is potentially more costly than just a pass or fail, but you could face physical injury or death.

For me, it started when it was my turn to drive on that racetrack. I remember, sitting at the steering wheel with my instructor next to me, moments before it was my turn. I felt a strange sense of calmness, readiness, and resolve. Upon reflection, I feel this was my pre-performance state, I was anticipating the moment to perform to a standard that would see me succeed. I also feel a big factor that enabled me to experience flow in this moment, was my positive outlook and optimism towards the challenge ahead. I have never been a nervous person, in any sporting championship, public speaking, or performing in my Year 12 drama performance. I've realised I would never feel any angst, nerves or nausea before these big public moments. Often, even when I was young and it was just my natural approach to these moments, I would always feel a greater sense of presence and awareness, both within myself and a greater appreciation and connection with the very moment, including the environment I'm in, and the people I am sharing that experience with. It would feel like a readied state in my mind and body, where I would be excited to celebrate all the hard work and preparation I had put in, and often shared with others, to lead up to this moment. The interpretation of the challenge ahead, enabled my outlook from the outset to be one of eagerness to perform, an excitement to be tested and challenged and the opportunity to showcase everything I had been learning. So much of the enjoyment for me, at a time when others admit the nerves begin to grow, was the anticipation in the days and moments leading up. I came to realise, this is my natural interpretation of the meaning of performance, one built on the appreciation for an opportunity to showcase my skills to the best of my ability, rather than being stressed with false and last-minute illusions of hesitation, doubts and insecurities into one's own true ability. Because my mindset and perspective into these moments is always one of optimistic anticipation, I dismiss any performance anxieties and interpret the sensations I'm feeling as a positive, thereby enabling my performance to be executed naturally and in a focused, confident state without expectations or distractions otherwise created through any misinterpretation of nervous or pre-performance debilitating stress. This is also accompanied with the confidence and peace of mind in my skill acquisition, that I have arrived at this place with consistent practice and preparation.

When the assessment started, it was a surreal sensation, a feeling of complete certainty in my ability. There was no way I could make a mistake, unless I went against all my natural instincts, but even that prospect seemed so far away and impossible. My senses were heightened so much that I could feel the warmth in my grip on the steering wheel. I guess that feeling had always been there, but I was in such a heightened state of awareness and connection with myself and everything around me that the signals my senses were sending to my brain were amplified. I was aware of the texture of the steering wheel under my fingertips, my muscle control was precise to the amount of force I had to apply to the pedals. The timing of all my turns and navigating obstacles were performed with so much precision and automatic response; even though I was in full control, it felt like every skill was being executed so effortlessly, and so efficiently that I felt like the car was really driving itself.

I completed the assessment in about 4 minutes 10 seconds, without hitting any cones, and obtained my 1B licence. I was very proud of this as it was an assessment under pressure with all the accountability on me to perform. Very simple, either execute all the acquired skills to the standard and within the time, or don't. I've reflected on this example of flow many times and asked myself what were the contributing factors that were present, that all came together in those few minutes to unlock a state in my mind that empowered me with all my natural ability and concentration, to perform to my absolute best yet feeling as natural, fluent, and effortless, even as unconscious as breathing. I think those key elements were the repetition of particular skill sets, that were progressively applied to more demanding and difficult scenarios. The pressure and expectation of assessment and knowing the degree of efficiency those skills would be applied, would determine the assessment outcome. My own interpretation of this pressure to perform, and how I could manifest that anticipation and expectation into a focused state of clarity, calmness, and readiness to perform to my absolute best, while letting go of the anxiety that may come with overwhelming oneself with the necessity to succeed. Once paralysis-inducing fear of failure is dissolved away, that's where a person's freedom of potential can truly spread its wings and fly.

Flow is readily accessible to absolutely anyone, and anywhere where performance, creative expression, authenticity, concentration, and connection is present. Whether it's painting a work of art, expressing yourself through dance, writing a book, standing on the top of a mountain about to snowboard down it, speaking in front of people or any sporting endeavour. Anything that is inspiring a person's best potential to be fully present, self-expression and connected to the task.

I've felt a similar flow in CrossFit competitions, where in the heat of the moment, the weights on the barbell seem empty or the efficiency your body is moving, or the intensity I'm able to push myself and not be affected by the fatigue, all this to a degree usually never felt in training before. To achieve it and surpass it in competition becomes a somewhat surreal and outer-body experience that occurs with a seemingly peaceful and unbelievably natural activation when all the necessary triggers are aligned. Like the potential you're experiencing has laid dormant until awakened. I realised that after my 'awakening' at Mallala.

Chapter Five

"The beginning of the best thing to never happen to me."

The conclusion of Phase Four, Driver Training and Out Phase, another glimpse into the world awaiting us, saw us commence Phase Five. The final phase to be completed at the Academy, before enjoying one of our proudest and most hard-earned accomplishments, graduation. Of course, the very next day after graduation, we would be back to the start line, tadpoles in an ocean of sharks as we would be crossing the blue bridge from the safety and seniority of the Academy and walking the streets in the real world as police officers.

Phase Five had a much more relaxing vibe compared to Phase Three, and even anytime leading up to the end of Phase Three. We had only a couple more decent sized scenarios and paperwork to accomplish, and final assessments including our OST final exam, physical testing, and the final theoretical exam, covering any and all of the legislation we had been introduced too from day one. This of course meant more relentless late nights studying in the library. However, the weight was lifted way off our shoulders this time, as the realisation of how close we were to conquering this last twelve months, a time spent in a place and an environment that becomes all-consuming of your life, effort, and energy. I loved every experience I had over those 12 months, no doubt my enthusiasm was nurtured by my resounding gratitude that I was now living the opportunity, the career that I had visualised and fantasied for years without ever truly knowing if it would ever be my reality. This was a gratitude I would consistently take the intentional time to bring to the surface of my mind and sit in its frequency of excitement and presence. This was an especially grounding strategy, that would help me to navigate my way through the thick smoky haze of pressure and expectation and be reminded of how much this opportunity had always meant to me. I would reflect on those many times that I would catch myself daydreaming about being successfully selected for the South Australia Police. I would visualise so deeply that I could feel the euphoria filling my stomach and throat in that moment I realised my dream was coming true. How much fulfilment and celebration I would feel knowing I had made it and would be answering my calling. I'm certain, this attention and intentional energy devoted to my visualisations of what I wanted to accomplish were a direct result to that reality eventually being manifested into my life, and it was the morning of graduation, that the gravity of that realisation, even though it had been staring me in the face every day, finally sank in with overwhelming appreciation, recognition and a feeling of awe in the moment.

I forget when I actually created the vision board, but I do remember I had done it in a moment of wanting to set clear intentions for the major areas in my life, and long before I was ever selected into the police. I had wanted to bring more purpose, and presence into areas in my life I was passionate about. The passion was always there, and this was a way I believed I could explore that passion even further and devote more intentional emotional energy to things I already loved and obsessed over. Looking back now, it was one of my first efforts in understanding my own sense of self-awareness, and the power of empowering yourself by setting clear intentions into different facets of your life. Bring a deliberate sense of purpose into your decisions and behaviours every day. Asking yourself, how do you want to be present in those moments, how do you want to exist in your own life, and what character do you envision yourself being as you write the best version of your life story. Through the power of imagery, these questions would be answered to myself every day that I woke up, anytime I was in my room, and I would be reminded of them every night I went to bed.

I had my board divided into four sections, each one with a small group of photographs or images selected to elicit and represent a specific emotion, feeling or experience. It's the consistent unassuming presence of a vision board in your life that makes it so impactful. I believe the regular visual reminder of intentions, goals, even qualities within yourself you're striving to raise, has a direct impact in eventually manifesting these aims into our life. The very idea of a vision board is to constantly remind us of who and what we're working to become. Setting those intentions in our mind every day. Even days where the presence of the board may be overlooked or underestimated, those images have still been looked upon, thereby reinforcing the deliberate behaviours and decisions we choose to make, to take another step closer towards living the life we envision.

One the four sections represented my future dream career with the police. I can still see the images as if they were still in front of me. I had an image of the

SAPOL emblem. It speaks for itself; a visual representation of what I wanted my life to stand for and the calling I was relentless in answering. An image of two Special Tactics and Rescue (STAR) Officers. STAR had always been the long-term goal once I was successful in actually getting into SAPOL. However, I was always very grounded in exploring this goal, I knew the two most important goals in my sights for the meantime were making it into police, I think I've established in your mind that this was a pretty big deal for me, and once this happened, working every day to build my experience, skills, knowledge and confidence to develop into the police officer I believed I was capable of being. The third image was a picture of a graduating course from the Academy, on the grassed-parade ground in front of the memorial, throwing their peak-caps into the air.

It was the morning of my graduation. After 12 months of the most intense and fast-paced learning and training of my life, literally the last year having been all-consuming as a police cadet, today I would celebrate by marching with my course in front of our friends, our family, Academy instructors, other high-ranking officers, and other cadets. We would all be officially sworn into the South Australia Police by individually marching up to the Commissioner of Police, saluting him, shaking hands with him, looking him in the eye, being congratulated on what we had just achieved and being presented with our warrant cards as we graduated from cadets and commenced our careers as probationary constables.

That's more than I had intended to write in that paragraph, however, it was that morning that I truly felt the full extent of the purpose of my vision board. As I was getting ready that morning in my bedroom, I can clearly remember I was standing in front of my vision board, getting dressed, and not particularly focused on it. It had been in my room, in that same position on my wall for way over 12 months. Most days I wouldn't look on it with much significance...but it was always there, subconsciously the first thing I would be looking at when I woke up, and one of the last things I would see when I got into bed. As I was putting my shirt on, as I looked up my eyes landed on the image of the course graduating, and throwing their hats in the air, I froze. My gaze immersing into the image before me as I suddenly realised; this vision, this image that represented something I had dreamt about and committed myself to realising. I was about to live in that very moment, feeling and experiencing the same emotions and euphoria, pride and overall accomplishment and excitement as those same cadets. I would be one of them in the exact same spot on the parade ground throwing my hat in the air with my course mates. The meaning of this moment suddenly brought me directly into the present and I stopped what I was doing as a wave of complete appreciation for the now, and its meaning washed over me. The power of the vision board was shining on me, as if someone or something had ensured that I would be facing my board at that very moment and that image would be directly in my sights to signify its manifestation into my life, on the very morning it was about to happen. I realised that every day for the last 12 months, and many more before that as I was progressing through selection, every day that image had been in my life that I had been focused, visualising and intently working towards it. Consciously, I was unaware of this most days, but I was thinking about that meaning of that image or that moment every single day to some degree. But subconsciously, that image had been reinforced every morning, and every night into my psyche so that my daily efforts were clear, and the intentions of my actions were focused towards what I was working for. Literally exactly how it had appeared to me every day, through its consistency and my intentions, that image and the emotions and milestone it symbolised was about to jump off the board and be manifested into my life.

The feelings, emotions and overwhelming present state of appreciation mixed in with realisation was exactly as I had imagined that moment depicted on my board to be. The sense of pride and service that surged through me on that day was electric, I really felt like a bulletproof superhero about to be unleashed onto the world. When I had first started at the Academy, probably in my first week as a cadet, we didn't even have our uniforms yet and were still wearing our civilian business attire, we got to watch a course graduate. At the time, I could only imagine what those course members were feeling and thinking, as they were at the accomplished end of an intense and arduous journey. The very same journey that I was only taking my first steps into. In that moment, that feeling seemed a lifetime away and now, after successfully passing every exam, every assessment, every expectation the Academy had of me. It was my time to celebrate a huge personal accomplishment and showcase with my course mates, the values that had been instilled, and at times beaten into us, in front of our family, friends and peers. It had always been a powerful moment to me, when you can welcome friends or family into an environment that holds so much meaning and importance in your heart. At the Academy, I had spent most of the last 12 months being schooled and trained in the ways of policing, forging the foundation of a hard-earned, and challenging career. This place was steeped in so many memories of my past 12 months, and now my family, for the first time, would step inside this world and see it, and feel it in its most formal and celebrated moment. The pinnacle of 12 months of intensive training.

The graduation march-out was a moment of true elation and pride. The ceremony and formations we would execute to precision had been refined since pretty much the first day we started marching, but especially in the last couple weeks when preparing for graduation was our sole priority. Everything else like exams and classes had all pretty much been finished. The parade had two other courses; courses behind us in their own training, who would march out both in front of us and behind us, so the formation had a more powerful presence on the parade ground. Also, members from the Mounted Division (the horses) would march out on their horses in full ceremonial uniform and flags to mark the occasion, along with the SAPOL band who, also in marching formation would play the traditional graduation song. This would be second nature to us, as we would march in time with their beats.

Standing in the driveway, our course in formation and dressed in our police best awaiting the commencement of the ceremony was a surreal feeling. I could feel my chest rising with every slow breath as we readied ourselves to march once the band began to play, something we had rehearsed constantly. Once on the move, as we followed the driveway around, we approached from the side of the parade ground, where the crowd of family, friends, instructors, and officers were all waiting. That feeling of marching onto the grassed parade ground, in precision formation, our uniforms clean and sharp and now absent of the blue 'cadet' badges as the traditional blue and white checkers signified our progression from cadets to officers, knowing all those eyes were seeing you for the first time in your full uniform was powerful, and for them must have been an overwhelming cocktail of pride, emotions and celebration. As I stood at ease in formation, listening to all the dignified speeches, the moment we recited the SAPOL oath as it was stated to us, I could feel my chest swelling out of my shirt and the sense of service, sacrifice and commitment I felt in that moment really did make me feel like a superhero to my community. That no matter what challenges, horrors or resistance thrown at us, I would face it without fear and selfless courage to the point that my safety and life was a necessary sacrifice for the safety and wellbeing of the innocence I was swearing on my life to protect. I was ready to uphold my commitment to the absolute very best of my ability, and

I would run headfirst into danger when everyone around me would be running away from it. On this day, the training environment I knew so well was now over, behind me, and I was graduating into the limitless unknown, a vast ocean ahead of me full of unknown but inevitable dangers and opportunities; my roller coaster had only just begun.

I didn't know it yet, but I was about to launch into the most confronting and equally clarifying journey of self-discovery and awareness that I could ever possibly hope for in life. Looking back now, many of the personal conflicts and realisations that gave me clarity, and guided my decisions later in my career, I would experience in the first few weeks of my Probation. This early in such a foreign and confronting environment though, I would dismiss them as unnatural because I was still new to them, I hadn't been exposed to so much enough to develop my skill sets and confidence as too know how I would handle situations according to my instincts and style. But as I'll go into greater detail later, these unnatural forces, feelings of distance and suppressing my natural elements as a person would eventually be conflicting factors that after almost two years on the job, I could no longer ignore if I wanted to experience my own sense of freedom and fulfilment. Sometimes, we have to follow a path, to experience the feeling of taking steps in the wrong direction to suddenly realise we were not destined to walk it. While serving in the police, and the highest calling to service and self-sacrifice I believed it represented, while this had been a dream of mine for more than eight years (that's before I ever got selected into SAPOL) I had to live that dream to realise it's not where my unique light can shine its brightest, and it's not where my full and authentic expression of who I am and who I want to exist within this world can fully be realised. Every day since, I have been filled with nothing but deep gratitude and appreciation for every moment I lived within the police. I have nothing but the deepest sense of admiration and respect for those devoted to the service and who have found that balanced harmony between living a fully functioning and healthy personal life, finding personal and spiritual growth, while consistently facing the rigors and unique stresses of the career. It's a life experience I will never forget and will owe so much of my deeper understanding as to who I really am, and the gift I believe I can share from living closer to my element. For this reason, and these milestones I discovered about myself through existing in an environment that forced me to face them, serving with the South Australia Police was the best thing to never happen to me.

Chapter Six

"Hindley Street...The street of dreams."

In the months before we graduated from the Academy, we had to put in our top three preferences as to where we wanted to be posted. Before I ever started at the Academy, and was progressing through selection, the only other thing I had wanted as much as being selected, was to serve on Hindley Street. Hindley Street is Adelaide's red-light district; it stretches from the western perimeter of the city, West Terrace to the middle of the Adelaide Central Business District (CBD) bordered by King William Street. Most of the city's strip clubs and major nightclubs are populated along Hindley Street, so Friday and Saturday nights, Hindley comes alive as crowds of party goers hit the clubs to shake off the week and party late into the weekend, and in classic Hindley tradition, usually fuelled by copious amounts of alcohol and any other substance that will ensure their inhibitions are thrown to the wind, and they can revel in reckless abandon and temporarily absent dignity.

I knew the reputation Hindley had; as for many years prior, I had enjoyed many reckless nights partying late into the early hours of the morning, usually throwing my own inhibitions to the wind, but always out for an innocent fun night. As I drew closer to graduation, a hungry cadet, full of training and knowledge, ready to be unleashed against criminals and eager to make my impact and presence felt within my community, Hindley Street was always the first choice in my mind. Actually, it wasn't just my first choice, I had decided it was my only choice. I just couldn't see any other option or preference where I wanted to serve; I hadn't even given it any thought. I've realised, this certainty in my mind has served me well over the years. It's what saw me persist throughout university, and it was a huge factor in my success in making it through SAPOL selection. If I can explain it to anyone, it is having the clear vision of what you're wanting to achieve in life, your next big career or personal ambition. Next, envisioning the path you have to follow to be working towards that goal, like seeing all the footprints already laid out before you, the path in front of you, and seeing every step you have to take. Then, and this is probably a part that some people may become overwhelmed by, or their anxiety and self-expectation along their journey takes a strangle hold on them. It's about completely letting go of the destination all together. Focus your energies, and your intentions on the steps in front of you as you move in that direction. Completely let go of any ideas of success or failure. Because ultimately, if you have followed your path with absolute commitment and excellence, whatever destination you arrive at will be one of peace and resolve, as you can wholeheartedly look within yourself and know that there is absolutely nothing else I could have done within my power or intentions, effort or commitment to arrive at this place. I walked that path with excellence and every footprint I left is a true reflection of my very best effort and concentration. Paradise is only truly appreciated when the anticipation of the journey and gratitude to get there is fully realised.

The chaos, anarchy, and intensity that Hindley Street was known for use to raise my pulse just at the very thought of it. I am an adrenaline junkie at heart, so this fast-paced atmosphere naturally appealed to me. As I had been told at the Academy, starting at Hindley Street would be a 'baptism of fire.' It made sense to me to come straight out of the Academy, and jump straight into the deep end, headfirst where my armour would quickly be hardened, and I could sharpen my steel as a resilient operator. I basically figured it would be the perfect place to prepare me emotionally for many of the confronting and graphic things I was about to see as a police officer. I took it as a badge of pride that no one else that I knew of had any intention to go anywhere near Hindley Street because of its reputation. Friday and Saturday nights spent breaking up fights, dealing with intoxication and the chaos that usually comes with large crowds of people looking to let loose. My thinking was, as explained before, someone needs to be willing to stand in the face of all that carnage and face it head on. Plus, as resilience is such a fundamental quality for police officers, why not strengthen it by putting it under the most testing conditions. I actually had to write a report, justifying the reasons why I should be posted to Hindley. This made it even more exclusive to me, and the more the place seemed like the last area a new Probie (Probationary Constable) should go, the more I wanted to go there.

The afternoon before we were due to receive our postings, our course mentor came into the classroom. He basically announced that two of us would have to go to a country/regional posting. If no one nominated themselves, then names would literally be pulled from a hat. You could feel the air in the room drop. He allowed this realisation to marinade in before saying that we are all adults and should be able to come to a solution ourselves. With that, he left the room to allow us to ponder what this meant. The idea of being posted somewhere we had no intention of going was admittedly, daunting. But in my mind, I felt a quick feeling of resolve as I realised if I didn't have any choice in the decision, I would still go into it with the very best intentions and excitement. We had all been grinding for the last 12 months and were eager to put all that training into action, so no matter where I was to end up, the unknown was a new adventure. The realisation was met with mixed emotions; a couple even became highly distressed, at one point stating that if their name was pulled, they'd resign. Thankfully, it didn't take the course long to come to a decision, and two of the girls put up their hands, saying they were about three quarters anyway from deciding to go country, so this situation would make that decision for them.

On the day my course received our postings, they were met with a mixed bag of emotions. Some were openly disappointed, and even frustrated. My head nearly hit the ceiling when I saw I would be going to Hindley Street. I remained grounded but shared with anyone who asked my elation knowing that another milestone step in my journey had been achieved. That feeling of floating, weightlessness when something you've envisioned and daydreamed about has actually been realised. I was going to Hindley Street, and the street of dreams would quickly live up to its reputation.

My first team I was posted to welcomed me warmly. I was the newest Probie to a team made up mostly, of other probationary constables. As I was at the beginning of my probation, I was always in the company of a senior member on the team, an experienced operator who possessed the qualifications to mentor a Probie on the job and guide their progress while assessing and critiquing their performance. This officer, a field tutor, was usually of the rank of either a constable, senior constable, brevet sergeant, or sergeant. The team dynamics and cultures of every team are always very unique and established. As my first team was mostly Probies; the energy and eagerness were always high. Our senior members were all easy to connect with and highly respectable. This could often be determined by their leadership qualities, their confidence and assurance as to how they managed situations and interacted with everyone from suspects to witnesses. My field tutor was quick-witted, with a direct and usually dirty sense of humour. He also drew a clear line in the sand when communicating with people. Assertiveness is a cornerstone in policing, and I quickly found if it isn't a natural trait in a person, with enough exposure in this climate, it would soon be forged. Some of his great lines, announced in his thick accent when someone was testing the range of that line in the sand, was, "Shut up or you're going to jail!" He was equally fair as he was assertive, and dependent on the attitude and behaviour of a person, he would show them the respect and patience they warranted. The best operators were always composed, fair and respectful towards suspects, but would make it clear they were the authority and would not be walked over. Even in the face of arrogance, aggression, ego, and intoxicated ego it takes a very composed, clear, resilient, and grounded mind to suppress any natural triggers, decompartmentalise your personal opinions about any insults thrown your way or actions you're seeing and suppress an inclination to meet a person on that same emotional level of intensity and confrontation. I discovered quickly that being confronted by this had no impact on me whatsoever. I'm impartial by nature, and nothing anyone will say or do, especially if they're not known to me, will really elicit an internal emotional response. However, I am guided by a very grounded moral compass, and I can recognise the damage and distress a person's behaviour and actions can cause, and when they are crossing a line. With these qualities, I found nothing anyone would say to me would ever be taken personally, it just went straight through me. In their moments of anger, emotions, hatred, and intimidation, or attempts too they were showing me their emotional weaknesses, their vulnerabilities and fragility and an inability to self-manage or regulate their state of being. Now admittedly, many of these people I encountered were suffering from mental health, or substance abuse, or commonly a combination of both. I always remained very neutral in these interactions, recognising this person doesn't have the capacity, let alone the capability to self-restrain or act against their behaviour and emotional impulses. In short, their sense of self-awareness, emotional regulation and even emotional intelligence were minimal, so, personal attacks towards me had no personal reaction. If a person is raging in your face, they've already shown a chink in their armour, a grandiose stage show of arrogance, ignorance, egotistical rambling to cover a soul that is perhaps deeply traumatised, vulnerable, insecure and lacking the psychological capabilities to independently function in their life. This, of course, does not apply to everyone and during my time on Hindley Street I would wade into an ocean of unique personalities and endless reasons for their actions and behaviour. In my first few weeks on Hindley Street, one interaction stood out that helped me truly discover the depth of my resilience and tolerance.

Everyone probably remembers their first arrest. It's an authority as a police officer that you carry, and it comes with a heavy weight of responsibility and justification. When you can decide with enough reasonable suspicion or belief, that this person should be deprived of their rights and taken, forcefully if necessary, into custody. The first time is intense, as no one likes or believes their rights can be taken away, no matter how obviously illegal their actions are.

On this day, my field tutor and I got tasked to a disturbance between a male and female, near a bus stop on a main street in the city. It was around knock off time on a weekday, so people were lining the streets after finishing work, getting ready to catch their buses home. When we arrived, there were already other patrols on scene.

A female was in the public phone booth, with officers already trying to interact with her. One glance at her, and it did not take an expert to see she was a victim of substance abuse, and undoubtedly a hard-lived life, something that for the remainder of the night, she would remind my colleague and I of, in between the verbal abuse and lashing out. She appeared haggard, nothing left but skin and bone, and leathery strained skin that appeared like weathered leather crudely and tightly wrapped around her frame. Her erratic, and unpredictable fidgeting suggested she was already suffering the effects of a substance. She would go almost internal, twitching and flinching and then rapidly lash out physically and verbally, and repeat. My colleague, another officer and I interacted with the male.

He appeared just as weathered as the female, and heavily intoxicated, slurring his speech and straining just to string the words into a sentence; plus the aroma of alcohol was a defining giveaway. To begin with, he was compliant, providing me all the personal information I needed. However, quickly we realised he just did not understand the concept of 'you go home, leave her now' as she is dealing with officers (his female companion). He would start to stagger away before returning and getting in the way, oblivious to the instructions, or the meaning of them he had just been told earlier. Eventually, as his presence was a potential antagonising factor for the female, and he was interfering with police executing their duties, the male was finally Cease Loitered. Basically, this is a lawful direction from a police officer, directing a person to leave the area, and the vicinity for an extended time as their presence there is causing a disturbance, or altercation, or it is deemed there is the potential for it. Failure to comply is an offence.

Despite the male's objections and repeatedly being directed to leave, he began to walk away. We did not want to arrest him; he just didn't need to be there, and the female's unpredictable and erratic behaviour needed everyone's attention on her. The officer with me and I then turned our attention back to the female. Not long after, I have turned to see the male close by and approaching us as if he was walking up to the situation for the first time. The other officer and I have grabbed the male, one by each arm, gotten his hands behind his back, while another officer put handcuffs on him. During this, the male was informed that he was under arrest for failing to Cease Loiter. He just wasn't comprehending what was actually happening. I escorted the male over to a nearby wall to sit him down. It was around this time, perhaps his hands being in cuffs, that made him realise he wasn't just walking away from this, that his casual pleas just to let him go, of which he had countless opportunities earlier, turned into verbal aggression, verbal abuse and anger towards me.

I would see this behaviour countless times in the coming months, to varying degrees of resistance. Some, so egotistical and narcissistic, with a toxifying victimisation and disdain for the world, that the presence of law enforcement fuelled a rage in them that would see no choice but a violent outcome, always ending with them in handcuffs. For some of them, once it was clear in their minds that their false sense of confidence and deranged ego and arrogance had failed them, would either continue abusing and insulting you, I guess as that's the only power they believed they had left, or they would fall into an emotional heap wailing and thrashing like a child on their first day of kindergarten after Mum has just dropped them off. My armour and unempathising outlook on these characters was strengthened after repeated examples where they would selfishly and without restrain, hurt, intimidate, abuse or frighten innocent and vulnerable people. While I have a natural love for connecting with people, and I always try to seek out the best qualities in a person, fascinated by who they are and what their dreams and motivations are. In policing, I quickly discovered that while some people are born into this world into chaos, and domestic anarchy. They can be so extremely toxified that having the gift, the blessing of life, seemed sadly wasted on them. There's no contribution from them, no desire or ambition to seek out new challenges and opportunities that would see them experience the fulfilment of self-development and awakened awareness. I would always hold onto the core belief that some of these characters, with the right interaction at a pivotal crossroads in their life, could have a profound awakening and realise a potential in them, that has always existed but has just been overshadowed by their life circumstances. Dealing with so many every day, you realise this would only be a rare diamond in the ruff. Cold, I know to consider this, but this is the unique underbelly that police immerse in constantly, and majority of society will never see the extremes even once in their lifetime that police are facing multiple times a day, let alone have to manage and interact with them for consecutive hours at a time while being bombarded with threats and verbal vomit that could make you sick. I will admit, as I progressed in my career, there were times where I would think to myself, *surely a bullet would save a lot of genuinely decent human beings a lot of unnecessary effort and hardships.* On this particular night, after arresting the male, that was the first perspective crept into my mind. So, as you can imagine, these are not natural thoughts, and the furthest thing from serving with a motivation to inspire through my example. My motivation to serve in the police was always cemented by a love and enthusiasm to inspire others, and to protect the vulnerable and innocent from evil. I thought there's no more powerful way than to answer the highest calling in service back to your community. In the most selfless, and equally dangerous role there is. This was a dark abyss in my thoughts and reactions to my new environment I did not want to stare down. Over enough time, I realised I did not want to find out what version of myself would exist if one day, I went further than just staring into the blackness, and actually fell into it. Looking back now, it was probably the first real instance where I felt a personal conflict with myself and the role, and the world I was now a soldier of service in.

After the arrest of the male, I verbally gave him his arrest rights. I'm pretty sure he had no clue what they meant as the entire time he was screaming at me to just let him go amidst the sporadic name calling and insults. Around this time, the female was taken into police custody under the Mental Health Act, meaning she was under arrest, but would be escorted to the Royal Adelaide Hospital (the RAH) for a psychological assessment by a professional. When this happens, police remain with the arrested person at the hospital until hospital staff takeover care and custody of the person. As I would learn, this was often not a fast process. In my opinion, why would it be from the hospital staff's perspective. An abusive, offensive person has been brought in by the police, and they remain in police custody until a professional is available. With so much happening in a hospital, an abusive violent person, with police officers watching over them, isn't posing a direct or uncontrollable threat. From a police perspective, it meant a couple less officers patrolling on the streets, and less officers able to back up their colleagues should anything happen. However, to the credit of both hospital staff and police, all I ever saw and felt was reciprocated was mutual respect and cooperation. When you're a part of emergency services, whatever area you're in, you have a unique understanding and deep respect for personnel in other services. As you all know, you've faced many of the same challenges, traumas and emotional chaos as one another. When you meet a paramedic, a nurse, or a firefighter for the first time, you already have a clear insight into what they're confronted with every day, just as they respect and understand some of the horrors you have likely faced. Without knowing someone personally, my natural feelings, regardless of how tired or exhausted I may be, was always to show them the utmost respect, patience, and professionalism. I found, particularly after a couple of 'code blacks' (by the way, a code black in a hospital meant a person had lost control and was being physically violent and was a danger to themselves and everyone around them; this meant security needed to make their way there now), that making the effort to acknowledge everyone's response and support, even just with a kind gesture of saying thank you and recognising their service, this mutual exchange could be a potent fuel for someone's motivation through the rest of their shift. I know this, because that was exactly the feeling I would get when an unexpected gesture of gratitude was extended my way. It might be the eighth job for the shift, but in that moment, it would truly celebrate the sacrifice, heroism, and selflessness of what I was doing. In the world of emergency services, heroes will never seek out gratitude for their actions, however, that small kind gesture can remind them of the very real impact their actions are having. And in a world cloaked in darkness, often filled with thankless ignorance, abuse and hatred, it is that small flickering light, like a candle in a dark room, that can bring clarity by offering a glimmer of what they're really fighting for and sworn to protect.

On this occasion, it was decided that my colleague and I would escort the female to the RAH. Once we got there, it was made clear that we would be in the presence of her pleasurable company for a very long time. Her mood had not improved, and I get the feeling she was escalating. Whatever substance she had consumed had now taken a full strangle hold on her. She would be docile, almost sleep-like if only for a few seconds, before thrashing about so violently and erratically; it's a wonder she didn't break any bones. Her verbal abuse was relentless and came at us in rapid waves of rambling saying any disgusting word or threat her frenzied mind could throw at us. This was also directed at any hospital staff that came into the room to try and talk to her or treat her. Eventually, my colleague and I knew the safest option for everyone involved, was to handcuff the female to the bed.

It would have been around six hours before my colleague, and I left the woman in the care of staff. From the memory I have of it now, she had just been sedated and had fallen asleep. But for every minute of those past six hours, my colleague and I were in the firing line of someone suffering substance-induced psychosis. This was really my first exposure, that I can remember, of a person in this state. You realise very quickly, no matter how genuinely helpful and good your intentions are, nothing you say is being received or even contemplated let alone appreciated. It's like trying to talk down a wild animal in a completely frenzied state…regardless of your intentions and goodwill, they would tear at your flesh if you let them. It's really a one-way conversation, despite her having plenty to say.

My colleague was amazing to see in action. He was completely transparent to her ramblings and insults and remained completely calm and courteous. He and I would even join in the conversation if she took a small break from her barrage of verbal bashings. It was in this moment, hours spent with a person in a psychotic frenzy, that I realised the depth of my resolve and resilience. I have never been a sensitive person who is reactive towards the aggression or insults from others. In those moments, when someone is trying to project their dominance through trying to undermine or offend me, I've always been very composed and very aware of the state of the other person, and most of the time their behaviour towards you is never directly personal, but it is triggered from somewhere else deep inside them, as a result of something else happening in their life. In that moment, it erupts, I realise I just happen to be in the line of fire at the time. Situations like this, I've always felt those heightened intensified emotions from someone else travel straight through me. I have no personal connection to that person, and nothing they've done has had any traumatic impact in my life for me to take their attacks personal, and loose total control of myself. I have no hatred or disdain towards them, so my behaviour in response is one of clarity and awareness. Self-awareness is a powerful filter in these moments, as you find yourself calculated and very clear about what the emotion you're seeing is. You no longer see an angry, raging person as intimidating or frightening, but rather you see the vulnerability of the emotional state they're in, as you realise this is a point where they have lost control. As I would see this frequently in policing, the emotions would appear as a separate entity in a lot of ways; the person they were coming from was merely a vessel for that entity to project from. To go even deeper and practice even more resolve is then understanding or empathising where this emotional reaction is actually coming from. Anger, intimidation, aggression reflect each other, subconsciously they're trying to elicit the same level of emotional reaction from someone else. Thereby, giving the instigator permission to turn the confrontation into violence and become physical. It's a lot harder for a person to sustain that fuelled intensity if they're not being invited by the other person, who is not meeting them on that level. In fact, so many times I would see doubt and uncertainty in someone who started out initially raging, big-chested and trying to stand over another through dominance and intimidation. Usually, they're seeking the emotional equivalent so in their mind they have that excuse to become physical, fuelling their inflated, or equally insecure ego. That doubt I mentioned before, I would see flashes of it when the person cannot make sense of someone being confronted with primal emotions like anger, who is just not reacting in the same way, either through matching that anger or cowering away from the intimidation. When someone presents very calm, composed, totally in control in the face of raging emotional intensity, it plants that seed of uncertainty in the mind of the instigator. Their mind is expecting a reaction, and subconsciously, they begin to hesitate and question whether this is a person they want to initiate with, as often such composure means this person is accustomed to these situations, and perhaps has the training and capability to handle themselves and others.

That flash of uncertainty when a person can't make sense of your calm state, that's all that is needed sometimes to deescalate a volatile situation. As long as you can maintain your composure and patience in the face of their anger. An officer, who I worked with on my first out phase from the Academy told me, "The best operators will remain calm, composed, empathetic, even courteous right up until that very last microsecond before they decide they have to take action. But, when you flip that switch in your mind, and you decide to commit, you make sure you are all in, bring the entire force of the fucking world down on that person, and they will never expect it or see it coming."

Back to my colleague, me, and our new best friend we'd connected with over about six hours. Of course, someone in a psychotic state, under the influence of a substance cannot always be reasoned with or deescalated. Their mind is no longer under their control, and is in a frenzied runaway state, unhinged by mind-altering substances. But, as I learnt about myself over those few hours, there's even less reason to react emotionally, or take anything personal. As police can find themselves in these situations for hours on end, it would be just too exhausting and detrimental to your own state if you're peaking your emotions just to meet another person and over investing yourself for no more return than your ego being fulfilled. Plus, if you're dealing with an addict, as we were, their abuse towards you, while being fuelled by substances, it's also coming from a lifetime of hardships, abuse they've endured, poverty and years and years of built-up resentment and deteriorated self-worth. Even when having to restrain the female, I was only initiating force for her protection and others, not laying my hands on her out of rage or my own personal anger, but merely because that was my responsibility in the moment to protect her and others from herself. The emotional feeling when having to be physical was actually very disconnected, even numbing, but that's something I'll explore in greater detail later. What I found very quickly over those few hours, was my natural resilience and disconnect towards that type of instinctive, primal damaged behaviour. It had no effect on me in the moment, despite reflecting on the situation after ending our shift once the adrenaline had subsided and I had re-entered my world. This would serve me well in my career too come, however, it would also raise certain doubts and personal conflicts in my mind as too how this may alter me if I was exposed to it for long enough.

Chapter Seven

**"Hindley Street...Overdoses, clubs, fights, and foot chases.
Just another night out on the town."**

Before I ever arrived on Hindley Street, I had the same exact feeling of certainty that I was meant to be there, as I had felt progressing through SAPOL selection. I had been on Hindley many nights before, partying with friends on a night out and when I was a Youth Worker, as part of an early intervention program to remove young people from the city on Friday and Saturday nights. So, I had gotten a glimpse of the environment that Hindley Street was for a police officer. I was already drawn to the intensity, and the reputation Hindley Street had, and knew what a challenge, and a learning experience it would be to be posted there straight out of the Academy. Its reputation of clubs, dealing with drunk partygoers, drugs, violence, large crowds of people and that sort of high-charged behaviour in an intensified environment usually kept people away from wanting to serve there. For me, all those elements and the shear craziness that seemed to come with wanting to serve there played to my love for adrenaline and excitement. My motivation was fuelled by the belief that it would be the perfect environment to satisfy that side of me, and it would be perfect to harden my armour and sharpen my steel as an officer by literally being thrown head-first into the fire.

Working nightshift, 11:00 p.m. until 7:30 a.m., on a Friday and Saturday night always carried an air of intensity and expectation. These were nights when Hindley Street was a living and breathing beast. All the clubs were open, and the streets were often full of revellers. Extra numbers, cover shifts, were rostered these nights to ensure there were more officers to respond and cover each other and the large-scale volume of people in such a small area. But despite this, we would always be patrolling the streets heavily outnumbered.

Friday nightshift was the first nightshift of seven. It was always rostered after about five days off, so you could be fresh and fully recharged, ready to launch into the weekend. As I was living in the city with a mate at this time, I could walk into work, which only took me about 15 minutes. Friday and Saturday nights, I had a specific routine to mentally prepare myself and focus for a long night ahead. It was very much the same as going through a mental rehearsal before a CrossFit competition. I would have a scoop (sometimes a double shot) of pre-workout, put my headphones on and play songs that would ignite that fire within me, and supercharge my readiness and alertness. Living in the heart of the city, on these nights, I would be surrounded by the ambience of the city nightlife. The sounds of laughter and excited chatter of groups of people arriving for a big night out. The distant tones of clubs playing their heavy base. I would walk through the middle of the city with my headphones in, unassuming but hyper observant to the vibes throughout the city, and the crowds gathering.

Often, you could resonate with a particular intensity or tension in the air. Something from the vibe and energy of the crowd and the aura of the night that told your gut instinct, this was going to be a hectic night. Even being early into my career, and to this environment, I quickly began to listen to this instinct, as most of the time, it never failed me.

These shifts quickly lived up to the reputation that Hindley Street was infamous for. So many of my memories from policing are as clear in my mind as the moment they happened, but there's so many blurred together; the specific dates and times are difficult to distinguish. One of the earliest close calls I can remember was running with my colleague (the same one I had shared that special night with the female in the hospital) at full sprint down the middle of Hindley Street on a nightshift to get to a physical altercation.

One of the many unique resources we had on Hindley Street was access to every CCTV scattered throughout the city, many of them spread throughout or around Hindley Street. Officers working the station could communicate to patrols if there was a fight, a suspect, disorderly behaviour, or any situation they should respond too immediately or keep a watchful eye on. I remember being in the station when we saw the incident on the cameras. My colleague and I bolted out the station, and as the footpaths were often full of people, responding to these situations that required an immediate sense of urgency meant it was faster to run on the road. Hindley Street was a straight stretch of road, only two lanes so usually you'd pick the oncoming lane, cars are easy to see from a distance and hit the nitro turbo boosters and run!

On this particular occasion, the lane with traffic moving in the same direction we were was gridlocked. For some reason, a taxi, which were always in large numbers down Hindley, decided to pull out into the oncoming lane, perhaps losing patience and attempting to get around vehicles banked up in front of him. Stupid, really, because it was obvious to see the traffic ahead of him was stopped, and he would be pulling into the wrong lane with nowhere to go if another vehicle was coming towards him. At this time, I was at full sprint when he pulled directly into my path just a few metres ahead of me. With no time to slow down, let alone stop, I ran into the driver's side front wheel panel and pancaked flat across the front bonnet. With adrenaline flowing, and being focused on getting to this job, I pushed off the taxi pointed to the driver and let some explicit words spray across his windscreen before running on.

At the end of the shift, when the energy and constant alertness starts to subside and the heaviness and fatigue of maintaining this state through a fast-paced eight hours begins to set in, that was when I began reflecting on some of the things I had just been through. This night, I realised, I had only been seconds and inches away from potentially, a much more devastating collision. If that taxi had pulled out a second later, he would have completely taken my legs out from under me, and the speed I was running, who knows how serious or long-term the damage could have been. In the moment, being fuelled by adrenaline and knowing instantly there was no injury, momentum kept me going, but the reality of how close I had come to something serious was not lost on me.

Policing quickly reveals to you what your natural instinctive reaction is too danger and conflict. Whether its fight, flight, or freeze. For many, even if their natural inclination is flight, or to freeze, that's something that will quickly be revealed and understandably when you're new to such a demanding confronting career. With experienced mentors who can recognise these hesitations and coach and support you through them, and a probationary whose devotion to the role is enough that they are willing to persevere and overcome that instinct, anyone can transform themselves into a reactive vigilante operator. All it takes is belief and repetition. In the police, this repetition can happen almost on a daily basis.

The fight, flight, freeze response is a unique and instinctive response. With enough training and exposure, what seems like an unnatural reaction can become a person's primary response. It's a subconscious, psychological and physiological survival mechanism inside all of us. When we're faced with danger, and our safety, or our life is under threat, very rapid internal chemical reactions take place to enable us to survive. For example, powerful neurotransmitters such as adrenaline are pumped into our system, providing us with a temporary surge of superhuman abilities that will either allow us to run away, to get away from danger, or prime our muscles to fight back.

Police don't have that option of running away, let alone freezing in the moment. No matter how terrifying or dangerous a situation may be, police have sworn an oath to uphold their duty and responsibilities to the community and put themselves in harm's way to protect the lives of innocence. When everyone else is running away, police are the heroic few who, with selfless intent blazing through their veins, run towards the danger and will put their own physical and mental wellbeing at risk for the protection of others. That kind of heroism is rare, and surreal to see when you're surrounded by people whose daily job is just that. That act of selfless courage for a person they don't even know, and sometimes, actually quite often, receiving no recognition and even abuse for it. Early on I was always in awe of this aspect. I would often look at my colleagues, experienced officers, some who had been in the role for over 20 years, and I would often wonder if they still appreciated the unbelievable personal qualities they displayed every single day to do this job. Or even if they still recognised how others looked upon them with admiration and even a sense of disbelief that they were able to face so many difficult traumas over and over, and still function with a grounded sense of moral clarity, selflessness, commitment, and sacrifice.

Officers in a single day can face more traumatic situations than most people will ever encounter once in their entire life. Beyond that, officers have to enter those situations, and make quick decisions, with limited information and find a solution out of all the chaos. Sometimes those decisions are the last thing another person wants, like apprehending a violent offender who would rather take their own life, or hurt anyone around them, or removing an emotionally hysterical mother from her children because the Department of Child Protections (DCP) have deemed her unfit to care for them. These were the heroes I was surrounded with every day, and while I encountered my own difficulties, I considered it the highest honour when a colleague would acknowledge your actions and response in such dangerous situations.

Foot pursuits would often occur every weekend. Usually during nightshift, on a Saturday night, when the crowds are out, and emotions and intoxication can intensify any situation. During my time on Hindley Street, I had about eight-foot chases, and not blowing smoke up my own arse or anything, but I got eight out of eight. There was so much I really enjoyed about the role, usually anything that involved excitement, action, and intensity. This was one of my major driving motivations to request Hindley Street for my first posting. As I mentioned before, the reputation Hindley Street had I thought would happily satisfy my hunger for action and danger.

Being in a foot chase was like nothing I'd ever experienced in even my hardest training sessions. The closest I could compare, would be in a CrossFit competition. All the elements are present to transcend you to levels of performance and ability that you rarely can achieve in training. Exceeding even your own preconceived capabilities and experiencing what many would describe as Flow State, whereby you're functioning at your physical maximum capacity, or surpassing it yet you feel every motion and exertion come to you in the most natural and effortless way. For me, in competitions, that could mean moving a weight for repetitions that anytime in training I would feel every kilogram of that weight, yet out here the barbell seems to float under my effort. Or sustaining an intensity that is reaching beyond your redline, yet it feels like an outer-body experience and the pain and discomfort just fade away until the event finishes, then you're suddenly reminded of the intensity of the effort you're pushing as your stomach feels like a wet towel being rung out and your lungs are burning white hot as lactic acid leaves a searing sensation through your muscles. All those elements, or triggers create an ideal setting for a person to exceed their previous performance abilities. Being in front of a cheering crowd, competing against other athletes, being on centre stage in the middle of the competition floor, showcasing the hours of hard work and commitment you've brought to the gym every day. This environment and atmosphere would always transcend me to new heights, as I was always inspired by the opportunity to give testament to myself, by showcasing to others who you are as a person, through your willingness to suffer physically and endure over and over and come back for more.

A foot chase on Hindley Street exceeded this experience again. All the elements to transcend your familiar physical abilities in training were there, however they were worlds away from being on the competition floor. The duty you've sworn to uphold as a police officer, driving you to pursue a dangerous offender who has just assaulted another person. The knowing in the back of your mind that you're running after a violent person, a criminal and at any moment that violence could be turned on you. Psychologically preparing yourself to be in a physical fight, because if they're running from Police, that's usually a pretty good indication that they don't want to be caught, and if you do catch them there's that chance that they are willing to fight and try hurt you to avoid being caught. This included any weapons they may be carrying or concealing. Running through the middle of the busiest street in Adelaide on a Friday and Saturday night with crowds of people all around you, sometimes chanting against you. The responsibility of knowing you're in a position to apprehend a potentially dangerous person, and your failure to do so could result in others being hurt, putting other officers in harm's way or further crimes being committed.

Unlike the celebration and wave of euphoria that you could enjoy throughout a competition, not to mention immersing into the fatigue and relaxing after an event knowing the work and effort was over. Physical confrontations in policing were just the beginning of responsibilities in that situation. Even during a foot chase, good operators would be communicating constantly over the radio, their location, the direction of the suspect so others could intercept and assist. Then once the suspect is restrained, providing a situation report (a SITREP), and then commencing the arresting procedures, plus concentrating on admin you've just acquired as a result of that arrest, or even being caught up in a similar physically intense situation later in the shift. If it happens to be a crazy night, you might go from one physical job to another, doing what you need to resolve that situation before backing up other officers in another one. It really is amazing what the mind and body can endure when you take away their option to immerse in the fatigue after an intense effort or even feel the effects of that exertion. What you're capable of when you're upholding a sworn oath to serve and protect.

A couple of my first pursuits remain crystal clear in my mind for a lot of the reasons I just mentioned. The first one I remember was during a nightshift over the weekend. I was in the caged vehicle with one of my teammates and our Brevet Sergeant. A call out came over the radio of a young male who had just threatened a male and female couple, potentially with a knife near Hindley Street. Reports came in that he was running towards Government House, which in Adelaide is secured by a high perimeter fence, and being a primary location, it is an offence under legislation to enter that premises without permission. Further information was this young male had jumped the front fence and was somewhere within the perimeter.

We were travelling adjacent to Government House down a side street. My Brevet Sergeant stopped at a path that ran parallel with the rear fence. As I would learn later, his intention was for me to remain in that position on a cordon, following standard procedure while other cordons were established to box the suspect in. However, even the police dogs couldn't have kept up with me. As soon as the back door was open, and I was let off the leash before my feet even hit the ground I was already at full sprint. I realised I wasn't running towards anything, I just had it in my mind that this kid was jumping fences and was running through the property so I could catch him as he was jumping the rear fence. Sure enough, about the time I began to realise I had sprinted towards nothing, I saw a silhouette of a young male running across the path ahead of me. On the other side of the path was parklands and garden beds with large trees, but it literally went from the flat walking path we were on to a steep grassy decline. Even running at half the pace we were, with the momentum behind us as soon as we hit that hill, we would meet each other at the base of it. Realising he was crossing the path and heading down the hill, I veered off the path and made my way down. He skidded into one of the garden beds while looking at me. I was thinking he was going to try double back, knowing that I would have to change direction and accelerate back up the hill. I roared out to him, "Stop right there!" It came out so loud that it even startled me, it probably informed any other patrols of exactly where I was. It must have startled the kid too, because he threw his hands up and stayed on his knees. I charged towards him, still very conscious of the fact that the only information I knew about him was he could potentially be in possession of a knife and had already used it to threaten people. With this in my mind, as I was getting closer I yelled at him to get on the ground. He laid on his stomach and, through the adrenaline and my veins pulsing with battery acid I secured his hands behind his back and handcuffed him.

Just moments later, my Brevet Sergeant came walking over. The young male was conveyed to the Adelaide City Watch House for processing by another patrol. Sitting in the back seat, the elation and pride of what I had just achieved rushed over me, as well as the still pumping adrenaline. While my Brevet Sergeant then explained to me, I was meant to stand still, and remain in one spot, I had just apprehended a suspect singlehandedly. While this was an important learning curve for me, about standing still, and the importance of remaining on cordon, being only months into my career, the satisfaction of the outcome and that I had responded instinctively in the way I did, running towards, engaging with, and apprehending a potentially armed offender was a victory I carried close with me. I had proven too myself that I had a fight reflex, an instinctive subconscious response to run towards danger. This was only one of the first times that this reflex would be tested.

On another Friday or Saturday night (who knows, they could all be from the same shift! Those many nights spent on the street of dreams all become one big blur). My senior member had stopped a young male, who barely looked 17 years old, because he was carrying an open can of alcohol. The Adelaide CBD is considered a dry zone, and it is an offence to carry an open container of alcohol. Funnily enough, if you have just purchased a bottle of alcohol and have not opened it, this would be clear from the cap, then enjoy your night and on your way, as long as it's not opened in the area. As I learnt from my seniors, it was all in a person's integrity and how they responded to us pointing out the obvious too them. For example, perhaps they're from interstate and unfamiliar with SA laws, if their identification verified this, and they presented with a genuine sense of being unaware and even apologetic, I would simply educate them on this, take their personal details and get them to empty out the opened alcohol. When you had approached people so many times for this same offence, your intuition would serve you very well in determining how honest the person really is, or if they're trying to manipulate their way out of a fine, lie to your face or just flat out stare you done as if what you're telling them, getting rid of their alcohol, is an abomination. Perhaps for some of them, who have just spent so much on a new bottle, being out of pocket is a huge inconvenience. A learnt behaviour that became natural for me through sheer repetition was show no hesitation or uncertainty in those not showing you respect or courtesy for your professional duties and the fact that I'm calling them out on something that they have blatantly done wrong, and even tried to cover it up. Ego and intimidation do not transcend someone above the law, and when you're carrying the weight of that responsibility on your shoulders, those personal traits become empty and hollow. A reaction from a primal being whose Neanderthal instincts are deeply entrenched, thinking if he puffs his chest out and bangs on it louder than me, that he's the more dominate one and in control of the situation. This attitude would either only dig a deep trench for them to fall in, or they would quickly be humbled. You can stretch your own dick out with your own two hands and tell yourself you're hung but in the end, it's still flaccid.

I was never really intimidated by this alpha-male type of behaviour, but as I was exposed to these egotistical interactions more and more, it became humorous to me when someone would be escalating themselves, especially over something so trivial, which honestly, if they just had some humility and accepted taking responsibility that they were in the wrong, would have resulted in nothing more than a caution (basically an expiation notice without any fine too pay). I am an action man; I do love the intensity and excitement of being physical, and being 6'3", hovering around 90 plus kilograms and training regularly in CrossFit and self-defence, I was always humbly prepared to handle myself and others. When I say I found it humorous, I don't mean I antagonised them, or enraged them just to push them over the edge. That is not in my nature as a person, and I wanted to give every single person I came across fair and respectful treatment and give them every chance to do the right thing, or at least practice some humility and come quietly. However, when it was clear this wasn't going to happen, I found myself recognising the situation, and what it was about to escalate into. As I encountered these situations again and again, I developed a small mannerism, I would feel a faint grin rise on my face, it was more of a gesture to the person that if they continued this way, I was ready to go to war, and was not persuaded by their behaviour. In the back of my mind, if they were only escalating more, and as I readied myself for confrontation, there was sometimes a fleeting moment of wanting the action to start. Feeling your senses heighten, and the adrenaline start to warm your veins; others who love this sensation will agree that you just want to unleash it. Sometimes, I feel like this would actually instil a sense of doubt in the other person's psyche, whether they were contemplating it or not but my presence and demeanour in a moment when they are probably expecting that their behaviour should be dominating over me; I just wouldn't appear that way. In moments of aggression and intimidation, or when someone is trying to exert that authority, it is often done with the preconception that it will be met with vulnerability and compliance or equal emotion, as one dominant individual is trying to belittle and stand over another. Like a shark sensing blood in the water, seeing this physical and emotional response gratifies their ego and fuels to assert more dominance. Take away that reaction, and seeds of doubt are instilled in their mind as they realise this person is undeterred, even unpredictable, or unreadable and unless this dominating person is certain about fighting, they will usually try disguise their confidence while retreating and going on the defence. Intimidation is seeking out dominance; it hungers for submission or fear, but met with composure and calm assurance, and its disempowered.

Another automatic response I found myself doing was getting up close to people who were trying to intimidate. It would come at a time when I felt I had been triggered, that their behaviour had to be met with strength and I would close in on them, usually with a finger pointing close to their face, and asserting my presence. With my size, most of the time, I would be bearing down on them, ready to engage, but waiting for their reaction. But like flipping a switch, my assertiveness could return back to instant calmness and respectful interaction if the person changed their approach. Even all the violent incidents I was in, I never carried any personal grudges or disdain for that individual. Usually those situations involved an individual damaged by alcoholism or substances, or mentally and emotionally fractured from traumas of a lifetime of hardships and chaos. Even if I saw them again, I would greet them and interact with them with my usual courtesy and respect, and often it would be returned. Criminals, some of them on the wrong side of the law since they were very young, will still recognise and respond to respectful treatment from an officer. They've been living in that world for so long; many would know in depth the processes of policing. "How long do you think the charging sergeant will be tonight boss? I know I'm not breaching conditions of my latest bail, but yeah that's a condition of my other bail agreement." These among many others were common conversations with those who have been in the game a long time. They know enough that the easiest path to follow is compliance, and when an officer is only showing them respect, the best thing for them is to show it right back. Of course, this wasn't always the case.

Anyway, back to my story. My senior member was speaking to a young lad who was carrying alcohol. He looked like a typical young kid out on Hindley Street. A tight T-shirt that he had purchased and was wearing in anticipation of one day being able to fill it out with his beach muscles, and slick blonde hair, shaved on one side but grown long and swept to the other side giving him a half fringe. Kind of like he had bought a Justin Bieber wig, cut it in half and then put it on, backwards. As we always did in an environment like Hindley Street, being surrounded by people, while your partner was talking with the person, I took up a nearby position where I could be observing all directions and watching my partner's back, and mine. I'm pretty sure the kid was just going to receive a caution, when suddenly, he bolted.

I had barely been looking over my shoulder when in my peripherals I saw the kid take off. I instinctively went after him, as he dodged between traffic and crossed over to the other side of Hindley Street. I took a more direct line and got onto the other footpath before he did, and then saw him appear further up the footpath ahead of me. I realised he assumed he wasn't being chased, because he slowed to almost a walking pace. By this point, seeing my opportunity, I was running like the T-1000 in Terminator 2: Judgement Day, laser focused stare on my target, stoic face and preparing to grab him and take him down to the ground. He looked over his shoulder, saw me and immediately broke back out into a sprint. What he didn't realise, was we were on the same side of the street as the popular Adelaide nightclub The Woolshed. At just the right time, one of the bouncers on the door, who was conveniently at least seven feet tall and built to match, saw the kid running and then quickly saw me. He raised his hand and pointed at the kid, all I had to do was nod my head. I kind of felt for the kid, because he never would have seen it coming, but the bouncer ran from the club entrance and blindsided the kid straight into a parked taxi. For a moment, the kid actually disappeared as he was engulfed by this man mountain. By this time, I had reached them as the bouncer stood back and the kid, probably in a complete daze, stood off the taxi and turned and faced me. Never taking the chance if he was facing up to me, I grabbed his right arm and spun him back towards the taxi and folded him over the front bonnet. I thanked the bouncer and realised I was alone, so I kept the kid restrained, my arm restraining his behind his back until my colleagues arrived. Suddenly, I heard my name called from behind me, and recognised a group of familiar faces, some of my old Academy course mates came running out of the entrance to see me enacting my duties. Being in the middle of it, I gave them a polite hello, but kept my attention on the kid I was still holding. My senior member, who had originally been talking to the young man, just walked up shaking his head and smiling. With his experience, he had probably weighed up the risk of pursuing a person who was only receiving a caution. Me, still being a naïve and overly enthusiastic Probie hadn't considered any of this, and like a puppy let off the leash when you throw their favourite ball, I had responded out of pure instinct.

I checked after and there was a serious dent in the side of the taxi where the bouncer had sandwiched the kid between it. I asked the young man later why he had run, and in his juvenile innocence, he said that talking to the police had made him panic and he just bolted. He only received a slap on the wrist, and a board-check into a parked vehicle by a seven-foot walking wall.

Other incidents had the potential to be more dangerous. Once again, let me take you back into the land of dreams on yet another Saturday night. This pursuit probably stands out in my mind the most. We had gotten a report of a group of people fighting down Rosina Street, a side street off Hindley, that was notorious for seedy behaviour. About five of my team members, including myself, made our way towards Rosina Street. We received information the instigator of the fight was a guy who now had his shirt off. When we arrived, there was a scattered group of people, and a few guys all with their shirts off. I grabbed one of the guys by his arm and began to talk to him. Suddenly, one of the shirtless males, playing it very casual, legged it towards Hindley Street.

Myself and my colleagues all gave chase. An innocent bystander, in his brilliant wisdom and heroism thought it was a good idea to step in front of our path with his mobile raised and film the event. One of my teammates ran straight through him. There's actually really good footage of this, from the bystander who must have uploaded his footage to a famous Adelaide Instagram group.

The guy had made it out onto Hindley Street ahead of us, and maybe thought he was clear of us (if they would just look behind them, they wouldn't be so surprised). I came out onto the middle of Hindley and saw him at mid-pace with his arms raised, as if he was giving his victory lap to the crowd. He realised we were still there and bolted again down a side street on the opposite side of Hindley. As he rounded the corner, I was only a few metres away from him, and was closing in fast. He ran between two parked cars, and as he had to deaccelerate so much, I braced myself for impact. As I was at full sprint, if I had grabbed him we probably would have crushed the rear of the parked car and probably gone straight through the back windscreen. He did a few shuffle steps, got around the car and accelerated again down the side street. Perhaps a couple seconds later and I would have had my hands on him.

This guy could run. He still had his shirt off so I could see he was obviously fit, built like a footballer with a muscular physique and tall enough that he could have been a ruck man. He managed to gain a few more metres on me. Like I talked about before, in these moments, the adrenaline and tenaciousness completely take over. My legs were screaming, and my lungs were in my throat, but there was no way I was even losing a stride, let alone slow down. We came out of the side street and crossed over North Terrace, one of the main streets that forms the perimeter of the city. He ran towards the InterContinental Hotel, on the other side of North Terrace, and started up a small incline before I lost sight of him as he ran behind a large cylinder pillar. I slowed down to a walk as I realised he may very well be right there ready to blindside me. I heard yelling behind me and ran back the direction I had come. He had tried to lose me and double back around the pillar, right into one of my colleagues. My colleague already had this guy seated on the ground. I went hands on and assisted my teammate in handcuffing him behind his back. This guy wasn't fighting back, or trying to resist, I could see he was breathing heavy and at one point, I heard him say after he was told he was under arrest, something like, "Whatever, I'm completely wrecked."

This is the powerful effect of adrenaline, despite feeling moments of fatigue and the burning acid bath coursing through your body, the level of alertness, response, and preparedness for danger and confrontation far exceeded any level of physical capability. Once the male was restrained, I attempted to relay information on my radio. There's nothing like trying to talk, knowing everyone on channel can hear you, to quickly remind you of how out of breath you are. Your voice doesn't even sound like your own, as in between gasps for air, the words come out in an attempt to sound as calm and composed as possible…while adrenaline is still surging through your system and your body is in a flooded state of fatigue.

I estimated the distance later. From Rosina Street where the guy had taken off from us and following the path that he and I had ran, to where he was apprehended, the total distance was just short of a kilometre. For that entire time, I had been at full sprint. The situation, the importance of apprehending the male, the duty I was responsible for far outweighed any sense of self-preservation or any discomfort I might feel. Even if I tried to sprint that distance again, I probably couldn't cover the same distance like that without the same sense of urgency and responsibility driving me. It's a powerful performance factor, how your commitment to something much greater than yourself can push you beyond your own capabilities, in the pursuit of an outcome that you know you're responsible for its success, and if you're not, it could be putting other people at risk. My mind in that moment, and many other incidents, and I'm sure this speaks for many police officers, was focused on the necessity to capture a dangerous offender, and that thinking subconsciously transcends beyond your own selfish inhibitions or contemplations. There is a sense of duty that ignites your selflessness so much that you're only thinking of how you can best contribute to this situation for a successful resolution. How can your strongest strengths be utilised in this moment? The thought of danger, or even harm to yourself, while risk assessment and the safest action is always paramount, you can always find yourself face to face with that danger, and if you're not prepared to invest your entire being through your physical abilities and mental stamina, the chance of someone else hurting you or others is raised even higher. The question then never exists of wanting to engage, but I have too on an almost unconscious instinctive level. I heard a great saying once, "If you want to take the island, burn the boats." For me, this couldn't ring truer than in these moments. Self-preservation, physical or even emotional discomfort, foul smells, blood, vomit, shit, extremes of human behaviour and trauma have to all be left at the shore, and when the situation demands it, you set them all on fire and charge onto that island without a second glance back.

Chapter Eight

"Conflict and confrontation."

Conflict and confrontation were just a daily part of life in policing. As I would say to people, when your job is looking for trouble, you never have to look far to find it. It was early into my probation on Hindley Street, that I first started feeling a sense of conflict with myself, between the nature of who I am and the demands and responsibilities of my professional duty as a police officer. To one degree, I prided myself in my responsiveness and fearlessness towards running into conflict, as I was driven by my firmly grounded moral compass that would selflessly and instinctively disregard my own sense of self-preservation, knowing that the innocence and safety of others was being threatened. Even more fulfilling was serving alongside so many truly amazing individuals, who all epitomised police values and displayed the unfathomable consistent courage that is so prominent throughout police. What I observed very quickly in all my colleagues was a selfless sense of responsibility to put themselves in harm's way, or in very uncomfortable scenarios to protect complete strangers. Some might say, "Well, that's just a no-brainer. That's what a police officer is expected to do," but to be a part of that world, and have enough awareness to appreciate the depth of courage and sacrifice that it must take for one human being to compromise so much of their own physical and emotional wellbeing for another human who is completely unknown to them, and in some cases is expressing raw hatred and aggression towards that person. The moral fibre and strength of character traits I observed and was in awe of everyday, that were practiced by my colleagues on such a subconscious level, got me wondering if they still take the time to reflect and fully appreciate, and be thankful within themselves that they have risen above most to exist in life from such a higher place of sacrifice and service. So many had been in the role for so long, I often thought if this was a realisation, they still afforded themselves, or if being exposed to so much over their lengthy careers had distanced the admiration and overwhelming awe that they have every entitlement to feel for themselves. Anyone who has devoted so much of their life, their time, their comforts, and their emotional development to serving others from this place, in my opinion, they are living as the hero version of themselves that, as a child, they would have looked up to with wide eyes, awe and admiration.

So many of the conflicts I began to encounter within myself, were born from the very nature of the role, that being confronting people and telling them off. Having to be the baddie sometimes, as I heard from numerous SAPOL sources. Sometimes, if we could justify it, this meant depriving a person of their very rights to exist freely and forcefully arresting them against their will. As I mentioned before, the seriousness of the offence was always easy for me to act from my natural state of moral values. However, there were moments when I would have to act against my natural instincts, as my duties required me too. I realised in myself; I am not a person who looks for or wants to be confrontational in anyway. I am a person who thrives on connection, inspiration, and exploration. I love meeting people, immersing in positive and connective energy, and building that trust and rapport that you invite them to share openly who they are. Beyond the superficial surface level and share with you on deeper and more meaningful levels. There were many occasions as a police officer where this type of connection and interaction seemed far away, and despite another person's resistance, attitude, aggression or anger you would still have to engage with them and enter into conflict. On Hindley Street, this would often occur in public, either on the street or along Rundle Mall, a stretch of road only accessible to pedestrians, that is the central hub for many department stores, cafes, and independent stores in Adelaide. It is home to the classic hustle and bustle of a city, alive with crowds of people and buskers or street performers. Where Hindley Street ends as it connects to the main street of King William Road is where Rundle Mall begins, on the other side of King William Road. Hindley patrols were responsible for patrolling, by foot, Rundle Mall. It was a common occurrence to have 'shoppies' (shoplifters) throughout the mall, plus suspicious characters, or disturbances.

There was always a sense of pride and presence when responding to taskings in the Mall, as you would quite literally have all eyes watching your every move and seeing why the police were present. As your energy and attention is focused on the situation, your responsibilities in managing that situation and all the persons involved, it was easy to forget that you were in the spotlight of every person passing by in the mall. The uniform was merely enough to elicit this attention. One such incident occurred whereby I had to respond physically, feeling as though my safety was being threatened, while on duty in the middle of the busy mall. This situation would later transpire to be one of the greatest contrasting situations in my career, one that reminded me of how important it always is in remaining impartial and seeking out and valuing a connection with another human being, no matter how violent, aggressive, or distant from this prospect that they may initially appear.

My colleague and I were patrolling, walking down Rundle Mall when two males walked past us. We were not responding to any tasks at the time, so we had no urgency to get anywhere and one of the male's demeanour caught my attention. He appeared to me to be intoxicated, perhaps his friend carrying alcohol raised my suspicions, but he also appeared to be agitated, like someone who was looking for anyone to give him an excuse to be aggressive and confrontational. I turned around to take a second look at him and saw that he was giving us the finger. I motioned to my colleague and indicated I wanted to talk to these gentlemen. As I mentioned, his behaviour concerned me that he may turn on anyone who crosses him, just looking for trouble.

My colleague took the male's friend aside to talk, while I tried to talk with the agitated male. It was very clear, this guy did not want to talk, most of all to a police officer. As nonconfrontational as I was presenting, sometimes the presence of the uniform would be all the trigger a person would need. I started just by asking him if something was wrong, and then trying to reassure him that I could see he was agitated, and perhaps he wanted to talk about it. Both of these were met with 'fuck off' or other less courteous declines. I stood at a distance from him, as by this point he was pacing, and I realised my mere presence of being there, and not leaving was working him up more and more. In this moment, I realised I had fully invested myself into seeing this situation through. As his attitude and demeanour were escalating, with no encouragement from myself other than simply being there, I knew I was committed and couldn't walk away with the state he was in.

I remained respectful, but I knew that my being simply a police officer was fuelling his anger. He continued to yell at me and say, "Fuck off, I just want to watch the busker." He stopped pacing with his back partially too me. I was a few metres away standing still, when he suddenly turned towards me with his arms raised and came at me.

I reacted by going on the offensive and grabbed him to the back of his neck and one of his arms. There was a bench only a short distance away, so I charged him towards it, intending to wrap him around the bench and restrain him. He's raised his foot and pushed off the bench, forcing both of us backwards. I have countered by using my right leg to sweep his left leg out, like a Judo sweep or if you imagine a horse kicking its back leg out, while simultaneously throwing his upper body to the ground. The countering effect of throwing off his balance like that, caused him to fall to the ground with me still holding him and yelling at him to get his hands behind his back. By this time, my partner had seen what was happening and came running over to assist, while I recall him saying to me, "Easy, easy." I realised my fight response had been triggered. I had recognised a potential threat to my own safety, and that hardwiring in me, in all of us was activated. Even though my reaction was to engage physically, my intention was never to hurt the guy, and I was never emotional or out-of-control, not like flipping the switch and going into an all-out frenzy of rage. No, my reaction was still very calculated, and while I had chosen to go hands-on, my motivation was simply to restrain him and neutralise the situation. In the second, he had turned to face me and throw up his arms, my basic primal instincts decided he was a threat, and it was either my safety or potentially being harmed by him. No emotions, just a neutral decision of self-preservation. I was very proud of myself that that was my instinctive reaction, and not freezing in the moment while someone attempts to assault me. I was never going to give him that opportunity, yet I recognised that his intentions, or the potential of that happening and protected myself.

Once restrained, two other members from our team arrived in the cage car to transport the male to the Adelaide City Watch House for charging. My senior member could recognise I had probably overreacted, when the situation was just an agitated male, which perhaps in the hands of a more experienced officer could have seen a different resolution. However, he supported my decision for the fact that I had made that call myself, based on my own assessment of the situation. The charges would be minor, just a disturbance, yet the male was irate. I couldn't get a word in with him as he loathed and scoffed at the very sight of me and refused to talk to me. I could appreciate that, given the violent altercation we had just been involved in together and the fact that he was already having a bad day and was agitated before he encountered me, so once we had him in the back of the cage car, my senior member, in his calm and composed manner, spoke to the male.

We transported him to the City Watch House and placed him in the padded holding cell, while one of us commenced the necessary paperwork and spoke to one of the charging sergeants. As I mentioned, I never held any disdain or dislike towards this male, I was responding to a person's behaviour and the situation based on my professional moral obligations. Perhaps, that is a unique insight into my own psyche, but like flipping a switch on and off, I was able to return to an emotional state of impartiality and respectful and courteous interaction within an instant. Even seconds after just being in a violent altercation with someone. Situational and emotional awareness in these moments is a valuable psychological armour that can protect yourself from acting in excess and from the exhausting weight of carrying a personal grudge against someone. In this example, I recognised the male was in an agitated passive aggressive state from no fault of my own. Yes, my presence and unwelcomed involvement was fuel to his fire, however, I was not the ember responsible for igniting his emotional flame. Even when things became physical, I was still very rational and aware as to the reasons why. His state of mind and loss of emotional control had escalated, and my responsibilities as a police officer obligated me to intervene and find out why and alleviate the situation in the interest of public safety. Naturally, the male would be hating my guts, not only because being restrained and arrested would be the last things you could imagine for yourself when you're already having a crappy day, but because I was the individual responsible.

These thoughts were still rolling through my mind when we had arrived at the City Watch House. The male's demeanour had calmed down by the time we arrived. Sometimes, just taking a few minutes' drive, alone with your thoughts and reflections is all you need to get outside your own head and let the intensity of those raw emotions fade away…but often, this wasn't the case.

When taking a person in custody to the Watch House, one Officer, usually the arresting officer will commence the administrative process, while the other officer keeps observations on the arrested person in the holding cell, to ensure they do not attempt to harm themselves or worse. On this occasion, I was watching over the male. I forget how the conversation started up, but it quickly took an empathetic and respectful turn from both of us. I could see he had had a hardened life; he had had his share of trials and tribulations throughout his life, but he was actually very self-aware and mature in the way he spoke and reflected on himself. He acknowledged some things that had just happened to him recently that had gotten him into his mood. He and his mate had decided to go out drinking and something had happened before he came across us...so basically, he admitted he was just having a bad day. He even confessed, again I appreciated what he was saying, but whether it was the truth? He confessed that he was never going to hit me, and he appreciated I was just doing my job. We spoke openly and I was impressed with his ability to emotionally analyse and verbalise things in his life, and where he was today, how he had arrived in this place in life. Once my time with him was finished, there was respect between us. For me, it was an insight into the power of impartiality, and the positive connection that can still be forged through an initially negative, and violent interaction. We are by our very nature connective species, we seek out a sense of belonging, value, respect, and acceptance from those around us. Our own self-worth is nurtured when we resonate with others and feel that our presence, our uniqueness is welcomed, and valued. In this particular interaction, he was encouraged to let his defences down, in the way of his attitude and aggression. I was encouraging this through expressing to him my impartial perspective, to reassure in his mind that despite what had just happened, I was not carrying any personal grudge or judgement towards him. There was space created in the mutual respect we had for each other, which was clarified through both of us having enough awareness to understand the reasoning for each other's behaviour. At this point, talking to him and having enough patience to listen to his own justification for his behaviour, I could empathise with his position, and when I shared my perspective, he respected where I was coming from, and I had acted on my professional responsibilities. This was one of the positive realisations I took away from what started out as an aggressive and volatile situation. Not every job that became physical had such a positive conclusion but I was always proud of myself for two main reasons when a situation had escalated physically. One was I never reacted out of emotion, I was never out of control or loss control and in a frenzied state of mind. I had always made that decision to go hands on from a place of justification and calculation with no emotional aftermath or regret if my ego had been driving my decision. My process of decision-making would come down to the fact that this person is noncompliant and combative, and without me making this decision, this person could hurt themselves, my colleagues, or get away and put other people at risk. Finally, my pride came from simply the fact that I was capable of making that decision in the first place. To be present in a volatile, intensified, and emotional situation, and knowing what is demanded of me through the oath I swore as a police officer, and I had enough belief, and courage to follow through with that responsibility, even in the face of danger and risk to myself.

This sort of courage is displayed by police officers on a daily basis, in any given moment, they sustain a level of preparedness and responsiveness that is hard to fathom in terms of the constant elevated emotional alertness and stress of the unknown. Something I am always in awe of, even when you've been a part of it yourself, but seeing experienced officers and this state of readiness appears so natural. One moment they can be sitting at the computer, laughing with a colleague, and the next running to their vehicle or out the station as a high-risk incident is occurring. To me, it was always fascinating that at any moment on shift, without warning, the switch in psychology that had to occur to go charging into a dangerous situation and then have the clarity of mind to make decisions based on limited information or instantly, depending on the chaos you have just entered. This is that unique psychological disassociation and stamina I believe makes emergency service personnel exceptional human beings. No matter how graphic, traumatising, or unbelievable a situation may be at first sight, they disconnect from the very instinctive and natural human impulses of shock or fear, and are instantly responsive, decisive, courageous, and prepared to take responsibility for the outcome of the incident by making tough decisions that may very well go against the fibres of a person's soul.

Going to a coroner's was rare for Hindley Street, or the Adelaide CBD in general. Basically, if you responded to a 116, this meant there was a report of a death, and you as the Investigating Officer had to either establish a cause of death from the person's doctor (if they were willing to provide one) otherwise, you and your colleague would have to conduct a full coroner's investigation, so the coroner could be satisfied there were no suspicious circumstances surrounding the person's death. If there were, that would gain the involvement of many other, more specialist SAPOL departments, as you would be dealing with a potential murder.

My first introduction to a coroner's investigation was also a great lesson into the delicate and surreal skill of interacting with the family of the deceased, who in this situation, just happened to be at the scene while their father was still trying to be revived. This was the long-time owner of a well-renowned bar on Hindley Street. When we arrived, his two sons and their partners were outside the bedroom, inside were paramedics still working on their father. As you would expect, there was a solemn mood amongst his family, but I found I could easily remain disassociated to the heavy emotions and tension, while being fully aware of their presence and the gravity of their situation. Sometimes in this disconnected state, it seemed a bit like an outer body experience. I could hear the words coming out of my mouth, my actions were within my control, and I was seeing and smelling everything around me but I still felt distant to it. I would describe to people, "It was a similar feeling to watching a movie, you're seeing everything like seeing it through a screen, or from an outside perspective. You don't quite believe it." This was especially true the more graphic or traumatising a situation could be.

As I was making my way past the family, trying to be as non-invasive as possible, one of the paramedics saw us and approached us. They quietly told us he was a high likelihood of dying, but it may not occur until later in the evening. Once he was removed from the bedroom, as it was a second story building on Hindley Street, Firies (Firefighters) assisted by getting a ladder up to the balcony, so moving the male could be easier and remain as discrete as possible. My colleague and I then commenced our investigation, which involved a detailed mud-map of the room, highlighting the location of furniture in the state we found it; the location the male was found, and his position, and anything that could contribute to the death, such as locations of medication, alcohol, substances. Any unique markings or injuries on the deceased had to be accounted for, and any prescribed medication was recorded and seized, highlighting the type of medication, its form such as capsules, bottle quantities, prescribed dosage, prescription dates and the prescribing doctor. The depth of notes to take was thorough, basically an account of your observations of the deceased and the scene as it was first found. Statements from the last person to see the deceased alive and the first person to find them in that state. No detail was overlooked to ensure the coroner was left with no doubt that this death was either natural or self-inflicted, basically that there was no suspicion of foul play.

I didn't have much extensive interaction with the male's two sons. I remember at one point one of them being frustrated and impatient, as we were having to instruct them to keep their distance from the bedroom, while the paramedics were still working on their father. This frustration, I can completely understand, as your father's life is slipping away in front of you, and people you don't know are telling you that you cannot be close to your loved one for what could potentially be their final moments of life. I was prepared for their emotions and behaviour to escalate. I couldn't hold any resentment or dislike to them as I was completely empathetic for the emotional distress and panic they may be feeling. Anyone would agree there is nothing that can get in the way of yourself and a loved one in need, and me being there at such a vulnerable and distressing time, and then these guys having to be told they cannot move about their own residence freely to see their father, that's a moment where a son's love for his father, that primal connection that overrides any opposing force that threatens to overrule that bond. I was there in a professional capacity, and I had to ensure the scene was not contaminated with people moving freely through it. I had to decompartmentalise what my civilian perspective may be, being completely understanding of the son's distress. However, as a police officer, I was thinking that perhaps one of them, or both of them are in some way responsible for this happening to their father. I had to see beyond the emotions they were displaying and think from a place of emotionless calculation, which was enabling me to analyse the entire situation clearly, including maybe their emotions are a well-rehearsed diversion to make me drop my guard and give them the opportunity to further cover their tracks to get away with the murder of their father. The thought even came into my mind that, knowing the father was the owner of the hotel, what if this was an attempt by his sons to eliminate him so they could take over the business, maybe this was the climax of a family dispute over business that had been brewing for a long time. All these thoughts, particularly having them while looking the grieving son in his eyes as he's literally seeing his father's life end. Yes, I understand they sound cold and disassociated, yet this is the cold-hard reality of police work. Whether you're naturally an emotional person or not, you have to be prepared to observe emotionally extreme and traumatising experiences and people from a completely neutral, observational, impartial and emotionally disconnected perspective. Not only recognising the emotions present and the place they're coming from, but to be removed from any reaction they may cause you, suppressing even your natural physiological and psychological instincts to enable you to determine where offences have occurred, what evidence needs to be preserved for the investigation, and what course of action must happen with all people involved. Being confronted with intense emotions and traumas in other people, particularly ones that have gone beyond the point of control in another person, like a frenzied state of rage or uncontrollable anger or grief, these naturally illicit a reaction within ourselves.

This comes back to those primal survival mechanisms we all have hardwired into our psyche of fight, flight, and freeze. When we see a person in a complete frenzy of anger and rage, usually our instinct is to keep our distance, and avoid them to protect ourselves from being the target of that rage. Just like avoiding a predatory wild animal, we go straight to self-preservation or protecting our loved ones around us. Same if someone is falling apart in front of us, overwhelmed with grief and heartbreak. We want to console them or be present in the moment with them to take away the pain their feeling and bring them back, yet the confronting sight of seeing a person like that can trigger us to freeze, our mind goes blank, and we cannot even muster a word to say to them. Perhaps this also comes from a sense of self-preservation, as we recognise a person who has lost control of their emotional state, and how unpredictable that can make them. Even if we want to be close to them out of good intentions to comfort them, they may react violently through the trauma and sheer panic of what they're experiencing. These are simply my perspectives and my own understanding after witnessing different emotions and intense situations. I understand there are limitless reactions every individual will have in these moments, but perhaps my own observations can clarify to some what they've seen in others. In policing, these situations, you're basically a calm and still force walking through the chaos and destruction of a hurricane where the violent winds all around you completely blow over you, and you remain grounded and clear in seeing the path you have to follow.

In this moment, I was initially intrigued why the sons were not more distressed or emotionally heightened. Despite their eyes being watery and physical signs of obvious stress and tension, they were understanding and patient with myself and my brevet sergeant, and were compliant with our instructions, and went to wait downstairs while we conducted our investigation. Once we were finished and were leaving the building, we spoke briefly with the sons and their partners. I shared my appreciation for their cooperation, but mostly recognised their loss and offered my condolences. They were informed that officers may contact them soon to take statements. As their father had not actually died yet, certain elements of the coroner's investigation couldn't be conducted, like the last to see/first to find statements. We had been told by the paramedics it was almost certain he would die, and most likely tonight.

My brevet sergeant and I returned to base to complete what we could of the investigation. I had my investigating officer's statement to type, which is a very detailed account of your observations of the scene, of the deceased, any evidence and medication seized. It's a detailed account of every observation to justify a possible cause of death. As the male was not deceased yet, we completed about three quarters of the investigation so whichever patrol who were about to begin nightshift would not be slammed with the entire workload. There are so many amazing, inspiring, and heroic qualities I remember from my time in SAPOL, ones that were embodied and personified every single moment amongst officers. I was always so humbled and in awe when you would see them actioned by members and done so in such a subconscious and casual way, like being selfless and supportive for your fellow officer, even if you did not know them personally. For me, one area I thrived in was feeling the connection and camaraderie to everyone wearing the blue. Without knowing their face, simply them wearing that uniform and upholding everything that uniform stood for drove you to throw your own life on the line if necessary, to fight for them. Any opportunity you could get to minimise some of the workload for a colleague, especially if they were at the end of a shift and were managing a coroner's or any large and complex investigation. There wasn't any second thought or hesitation in my mind and while it would never happen of course, but that level of commitment would have drove me to do a back to back shift if it was required. Thankfully, that was never asked of me as I can only imagine what state of delirious fatigue hours on patrol like that could feel like. I was always so appreciative when others would put your needs before their own and be so casual about that gesture. In my opinion, selflessness was a natural instinct amongst all officers, and I say instinctive because you would see them practice it to the highest standard, without pause for their own immediate needs or concerns. To them, maybe it was so matter of fact or just what the job requires but to me I never took for granted the depth and meaning of that type of heroism, someone who will stand before all others in the face of destruction and evil, with self-preservation the furthest thing from their mind and push back. Selflessness can come in many different forms and degrees, but policing, with the high risks involved, the extreme stresses officers are exposed too and coming back every single day to face them again and again embodies the true extent of how selfless a person can be.

One of the last jobs I can remember on Hindley Street is still one that I just cannot believe actually happened. We were tasked to the Dog and Duck, a central nightclub in the heart of Hindley Street. It must have been a Friday or a Saturday night, because I remember all the usual crowds and partygoers were out and about, and the club was cranking. We were taken through the front entrance by security and shown to one of the main dance floors, which was crowded. There, laying on the floor was a large elderly woman; she had to be in her sixties, dressed in a leopard-patterned scarf or top, and bright white hair. She was easily noticeable, and as security explained, she had been refused service because she was heavily intoxicated. She then started to abuse bar staff, and any security that came near her. Her act now, as they told us, was playing possum and avoiding at all costs to be thrown out. She was off to the side of the dance floor, but we were all in full view of everyone. I initially tried to speak to her, even over the deafening volume of the music. She would remain motionless, until we tried to sit her up, or move her, and she would lash out. Quickly, my colleague and I knew that she was not going to be cooperative in any way, and because she was making it as difficult as possible to get her off the ground and sit her up, let alone to her feet, we each grabbed an arm and through the middle of a crowded dance floor, down the main hall and out the front entrance past the line, we dragged this elderly woman by her arms. It was at the moment of dragging her through the dance floor, through a crowd of partygoers, smoke, loud dance music, strobe lights and other pretty flashing colours, that the surreal nature of dragging a grandmother through this scene, seemed so ridiculous. As a police officer, with no limitations as too what you may encounter, you can be in the middle of a crazy situation, but there's almost a filter in your mind that tells you that this is so ridiculous that any realisation of this even being real doesn't fully sink in.

Once we had her outside, and finally in the backseat of the cage vehicle, we tried speaking with her. For some reason, she was more compliant with one particular officer, so it was best to step back and let them coerce her to comply. When she was speaking, she had an air of entitlement, and spoke with a pompous upper-class drone, the way a self-indulged wealthy person with too much ego and time on their hands would speak down to someone who in their eyes was beneath them. Probably because she was an elderly woman, so giving her the chance to be respectable and sit her in the back seat, rather than in the rear cage, might seem reasonable. She quickly showed she was anything but a humble soft-spoken grandma. She lashed out a couple times in her drunken state, and I remember at one point, one of my female colleagues was trying to talk to her, while the woman was seated in the backseat. She has taken a swing at my colleague, and amongst the heated reactions, I remember reaching over my female colleague and grabbing a clump of the woman's hair. By this point, I had been dealing with her defiance from the beginning, and her taking another shot at one of my colleagues, when we were all just trying to care for her, was enough. Admittedly, my sympathies for her were low. My colleague must have grabbed the woman too and pretty quickly we had her out of the vehicle, on the ground again and then assisted her into the rear of the cage. We took her to the sobering up unit in town, where she could be cared for, watched over and stay the night to sleep off her intoxication. Once we ran checks on her, she was a troublesome alcoholic who was dealing with a multitude of mental health problems, and this sought of self-destructive reckless behaviour was common for her. I always tried my best, to extend my tolerance despite whatever threats, insults, aggression, ego, and arrogance have been thrown my way to give anyone I was dealing with the support they needed. Even once my attempts were foregone, I just use to accept my efforts in this moment are not being well received, and you have to get on with the job. When someone's own self-respect is deeply diminished, and they are projecting out on you or people around you, that's not something to ever take personally, understanding that that single insult or aggressive behaviour is being fuelled from years of emotional destruction, self-sabotage, debilitating trauma and abuse. However, when people are at risk of being hurt, simply for trying to do right by another and care for them, there is a point where your empathic tolerance is set aside, and you have to intervene with force to ensure no one, including that person is going to get hurt.

Reading over these chapters, to finalise everything I have already included, actually brings to the surface stories and situations I didn't remember the first time through. This one about the elderly woman in the nightclub, strangely brought to mind a completely unrelated story. It was the description of what self-sabotage, diminished self-worth and potentially mental health can do to a person that reminded me of the following. My partner and I were tasked to an incident of a male wearing black who had just threatened a person, potentially with a syringe. To me, being injured with a syringe would be just as vile, and just as dangerous as being spat on by someone carrying a transmittable disease. An infection like that can change an officer's life, and impact how they're affectionate and intimate with their loved one, plus I'm sure, and endless flood of other physical and psychological impacts.

Sometime during our time getting to the last known location that the male was seen, a specific patrol in SAPOL came up on the radio, to inform us and comms that they were in the area and would support us. This patrol have the freedom to go to any district they like, like a mobile back up who can provide reinforcements wherever they may be needed. My partner and I pulled up at the top of Rundle Mall. It was night-time, so there were few people around. This particular field tutor I was with had been encouraging me to take the lead more in situations, so he would simply ride shotgun so to speak and allow me to handle things and make decisions. But as my seniors and field tutors said, they were always there to steer us (Probies) back on the right path if we started to stray and jump in if we really shit the bed. We sighted a large male wearing all black. His behaviour alone appeared sketchy, and I had a good feeling this was our man. I approached cautiously, knowing he may have concealed the syringe, or any other object he might be carrying. Keeping my distance, I tried asking the male questions, and getting more clarity as to the situation. He was worked up and bouncing around. I remember I was a few metres from him, and had one hand up, like you would if you're carefully trying to calm an agitated dog. He turned to me, still bouncing and muttering, and took on a fight stance, raising his fists up near his head. I realised this was going to turn physical. What the male couldn't see but I could out of the left corner of my eye, was the patrol backing us up had arrived. Without taking my attention off the male, I could see a large officer, strongly built and who would have towered over me (I'm about six foot three) get out of the vehicle and quickly, but silently come up behind the male. Like seeing into the future, I kept talking to the male, keeping his intent on me. He never saw it coming. The large officer wrapped one arm around the male's neck and slammed him to the ground. I ran in and jumped on the legs of the male, locking them up in a leg lock, while the officer handcuffed his hands behind him. As it turns out, this male wasn't that bad to deal with. He had regular dealings with police over many years, and was suffering numerous psychological disorders; he just had difficulty regulating his own emotions in any given situation. Months later, I actually encountered him again when I was posted at Holden Hill. We had been called to Modbury Hospital, because a male was going off in the reception area. I recognised him straight away, and knowing how that last interaction had gone, knew we could have our hands full, but this time he was easily talked down, and we were obliging enough to even give him a lift home. The hospital had just wanted him to leave. He even remembered me from that earlier encounter in the city and was gracious and thankful when we dropped him off. Surprising how the attitudes of humans towards one another can vary so much in different situations, simply by catching them in a different frame of mind.

Chapter Nine

"Welcome to Holden Hill."

My time on Hindley Street had truly been a baptism of fire to the world of policing. While over time, there were some elements of policing that didn't come naturally, and my mentors were pushing and supporting me to improve, I had no desire to move to another station or another district. I had wanted to be at Hindley Street long before I was even selected to attend the Academy, and despite personal conflicts arising within myself about the demands of the job, I was committed to immerse myself wholeheartedly into this journey and become the very best officer I believed I had all the potential to be. That meant, improving in some of those areas identified by my field tutors and successfully completing my probation period. Maybe, in some ways, I put too much pressure and expectation on myself, as I did what I had to to come into each shift mentally prepared to excel and to perform to the potential I believed I had within this job. Looking back, there was probably many times that I did not push myself out of concern for making a mistake or a serious fuck up. When your decisions carry so much responsibility and possible consequences, these thoughts go through your mind, but my senior members were always very open about the importance of stepping up and taking charge, under the guidance of them, as those moments were where the greatest progress and lessons came. As one sergeant told me, your senior colleagues and field tutors will never let you reach a place where you're completely shitting the bed. If they see your way off the mark, they are there to keep you on the right path. A few skid marks on the bed sheets are fine, it's expected in probation but painting the bed and the bedroom with an explosive coat of brown is not.

When I was called into one of the offices to speak to a couple of the probationary constable program coordinators, I wasn't even anticipating the news they were going to drop on me. They were a couple of sergeants who oversaw all the probationary constables in the Eastern District. One of them I had known from the Academy, and I had a great deal of respect for both of them, obviously their experience but who they were by nature, they were genuinely caring and invested in your wellbeing and development as a probationary and were always approachable to discuss anything on any level. Their commitment was to you, to your progress and development through the program and ensuring any struggles along the way could be addressed and a resolution to how best to support you was found.

As I was walking towards the office, I saw my team sergeant, and brevet sergeant both standing by the doorway. Both had the same look on their face, kind of a blend of stun and concern. I sat down with them, and the other two sergeants announced to me that I would be getting transferred to Holden Hill station. I had assumed this meeting was more general probie stuff, or maybe something about my progress, but I wasn't ready for this. The initial reaction was one of surprise, naturally, but I found I was instantly optimistic. I never wanted to express to my seniors any frustration or show cracks in my armour, whether it was warranted or not in expressing it, strength to me was through resilience and that no matter what they told me or made me do that I would take it on with enthusiasm and optimism and an attitude for opportunity.

Holden Hill is a north-eastern suburb about 20 minutes from the Adelaide CBD. It's surrounded by numerous suburbs; some being populated by the lower socioeconomic demographic. There's a lot of housing projects and cheap rentals scattered all around the area. From suburb to suburb, there can be a distinct variation from the suburban demographic, but like any metro-suburban police station, some hot pockets attract more police attention than others. Holden Hill Police Station is more of a police complex, a large facility that is the base for not only general patrols, but specialist units like Traffic, Criminal Investigation Branch (CIB) and Crime Scene Investigation (CSI) just to name a few.

I was about to be introduced to a completely foreign environment. Not just as a police officer, but me personally. All my life I had lived down south, only venturing as far as the city or suburbs along the coast like Glenelg and Brighton. Never in my life, professional or personal, did I have any reason to venture into the northeast. I would also quickly realise that while my time on Hindley Street had exposed me to a lot of extreme circumstances and human behaviours, developing my confidence and presence as an operator. What I had no experience in was suburban policing. Which in comparison to policing in a very unique and specific environment as Hindley Street, and the surrounding CBD, the suburbs presented an array of new skills that were invaluable to a police officer.

I was now the newest member to Team Two. The experience across this team was impressive, as majority of the members had many years of policing under their belt. For some of them, most of that experience, if not all was in Holden Hill. However, none of them had any experience on Hindley Street. As I was about ten months into my probation, I feel like some of them deep down, felt like my development overall should be further along, but as I would calmly inform them if I happened to be getting a grilling for something, being on Hindley Street I just hadn't been exposed to some things, even some essential fundamental skills in policing like driving or navigating. On Hindley, the most driving we would do was conveying a suspect in the cage vehicle to the City Watch House or getting to other locations within the city. But due to the congestion of the CBD, high risk driving, even to urgent taskings was pretty rare, there was just too much risk with city traffic, intersections and pedestrians.

Out in the suburbs, so much of your shift can be spent driving, or being a passenger and covering in excess of 100 kms sometimes. I hadn't done any serious driving since our training at the Academy, but it was a skill I would get daily practice in. From basic patrolling and traffic stops, to responding to high risk taskings that require Urgent Response Driving (URD) to get to them, and then, of course, being a part of pursuits of a suspect vehicle.

Being a passenger meant you were responsible for navigating, operating the tablet that received all taskings, communications, and you could access all police systems to conduct vehicle, licence, and address checks. Plus, both of you were constantly alert, scanning for any traffic offences, or anything that would require police attention.

Early into my time at Holden Hill, my introduction to driving and navigating skills was tested, with a laughable result. I can laugh about it now, but at the time, it was pretty fucking serious. At the time, it may have seemed serious given the urgency of the situation, but when you come out of it with no one being hurt, no property damaged and only a lesson to take away from it, it does make for a funny story to tell later.

On this particular day, I was riding passenger and my field tutor was driving. He was always entertaining to work with and a patient mentor, yet being Irish, he naturally had that burning Irish fire beneath the surface, and when the situation called for it, that fire would burn bright. I worked with colleagues from all different backgrounds, but it was always entertaining working with Irish and Scottish officers (one of my Brevet Sergeants on Hindley Street was Scottish). When they had to be assertive and escalate their voice, often their accents would follow and become more pronounced. There's nothing like hearing an angry Irishman or Scotsman barking at the top of their lungs. On this occasion, while I feel he did contain himself pretty well, and directed it to me as a lesson to be learned, I could tell that fire was burning to light up.

We received a Grade One response tasking, which means going lights and sirens, URD and getting there as fast as possible because there is an imminent threat. Apparently, a woman had been on the phone to police, saying she heard sounds like someone trying to break into her house, where she was at the time and then the phone call got cut off. From memory, there were other patrols responding too, and thankfully they were. I got the address of the call and typed it into the map system to navigate us there. When you're under pressure, where time and speed are essential, and your response time could be the deciding factor between whether someone gets away, is seriously injured or worse, and you have absolutely no idea where you currently are, put all those factors together and your thought process and problem solving can get a little fractured. My colleague, who probably had one of the most assertive driving styles when going URD, was barking at me to find the place. I admit I was trying to rush rather than centre myself and be efficient. What I didn't realise was that in my haste, I had tapped the screen in a way that selected another address on the map. Not looking at the screen at the time, or being familiar enough with surrounding suburbs and locations, I didn't see the change.

We arrived at a quiet, unassuming, and undisturbed two storey house. In these scenarios, if an intruder is on scene or has forced entry, your senses are already making determinations when you arrive; you're looking for any visible signs of disturbance or damage to the house. Also, you're listening for sounds coming from inside, yelling, screaming or crashing sounds of things being thrown around. At this house, we saw and heard nothing. We've pulled up and both jumped out the car running towards the house. The front door was locked so my colleague pushed open the side gate and ran into the side yard, looking for a possible way in. It was at this time, I was realising what I had done, as I had a flash of what the caller's address was, and where we had arrived. I quickly told my partner who gave me a surprisingly subdued mouthful, and we spoke about it further when we returned to base. Just as he had told me, thankfully, we hadn't damaged anything, like kicking in a door or smashing a window to force entry. SAPOL would be covering every cent of the damage repairs, on my behalf, of course. However, this was a valuable lesson for me in just how vital always knowing where you are, always having your bearings and being familiar with your local surrounding suburbs was for an officer. When a task comes through where an imminent threat exists, or life is at risk, every second you're not there is one more second for the worst possible outcome to occur. The most serious call that can come through over our radios, in my opinion, would be an 801, which is code for an officer in trouble. I have only been involved in a few of these, but if there is ever a more potent example of the depth and strength of camaraderie that is forged between officers; they are truly amplified in these moments.

I obtained strategies to develop and heighten my sense of awareness and my bearings in and around Holden Hill. While North, South, East and West are basic foundational directions, they can be confusing as hell to remember and switch between when you're constantly changing directions and you're not familiar with the area. On this team, I had five very experienced officers and field tutors. All of them bringing their own personality, experience, and ways of doing things to the role and to my development. I always saw this as a massively beneficial opportunity for my own learning and progression. Early at the Academy, they told us when we are on Out Phase, and throughout our probation, we will see the best and worst in the job. Those officers who excel in the role, go above and beyond in executing their procedural correctness, professionalism and depth of detail and standard in every aspect of the job. Then of course, there are some who perhaps get away with the minimal effort, or not taking the initiative themselves. However, in my opinion after seeing it first hand, these examples were few and far between, and if I ever heard stories about others, I would never go into any interaction with a preconceived judgement or assumption towards their performance. Until I am satisfied through seeing their consistent pattern of substandard performance or avoidance of extra or more challenging work, I will always give them the benefit of the doubt and presume that someone else's perspective of them may be completely different to my own. Perhaps another's perspective of someone has been formulated from a personal place. Maybe one personality just doesn't resonate with another, and no matter what that person does in the eyes of the other person. Their methods are never fully understood or even appreciated, simply by the fact that one perspective can see the same problem and same situation different to another, and their process of finding a solution is different. I'm a firm believer in never presuming one is wrong over another; an open and awakened mind will value the contribution of another's perspective, as it broadens their own ability to see and understand things. This is the sign of an emotionally intelligent and mature mind, one that values the position, experience, and perspective of another over their own ego and ways of seeing things. Through this patient openness, respectfulness to show others that their unique insights are valued and willingness to invite others to contribute and share their own individuality, a solution can always be achieved, and perhaps in an even more efficient means than if one mind or method is dictating all the decisions. These are one of the foundations to an emotionally aware, and egoless person, whose hunger and desire to find that solution is of course strong, yet they have the clarity of mind, the awareness and understanding of the experience and strengths of those around them, and the humbleness to recognise that their own methods and understanding of something may be expanded on by a fresh perspective. Of course, not all minds are wired this way, and in a policing environment, where your decisions and actions carry great responsibility and potential consequences, it may be hard for some to accept a different insight to something they have been doing for a while, and in their mind, works. Just like they consistently reminded us about at the Academy, I remained open-minded and respectful to my colleagues, most of them with years of experience in the role, and naturally, I would identify certain practices and methods that resonated with me, as I saw the positive impact it had, and it was a way of doing things that were aligned with my own natural perspective and values. Sometimes, I would see examples of decisions or actions I just didn't agree with, and I would see the value in them for my own development, reminding myself of the potential I believed I had in being an officer, one that was aligned to my personal values and code of ethics and commitment to the service. With these reminders, I would take the good and recognise the bad, but be equally grateful for the contribution all of these examples had to my development, as I forged my way building myself into the calibre of officer I truly believed I could be.

Back to those strategies. As it was identified, by myself and my field tutors, that my high risk driving and navigational abilities were not well developed, they all shared with me their own strategies to help me upskill. Sometimes it would be testing my awareness at any given moment, by asking me what road we were on, and what direction were we now travelling. Many a times, I would stumble and studder or simply submit to defeat, and say I don't know, braced for their deep sigh of frustration, that was always followed up with constructive feedback. Overtime, my awareness and bearings improved, naturally when you're patrolling throughout the same area day after day and travelling on the same roads regularly. Some of the best advice I received was landmarking. Scattered all over our area were easily identifiable landmarks including intersections, schools, and shopping centres just to name a few. Once the location of these were familiar, your bearings and directions improved. One of the most effective that was shared with me, when I was still struggling with my ABCs…I mean, my North, South, East and West, was so obvious that it was clearly hiding in plain sight. One day while patrolling, my field tutor goes, "What direction are we going?" When I couldn't respond quickly, he then goes, "Which way is the city? Then which way are the hills? Just think, anytime we're city bound, we're travelling west. Everything else should seem clear just from that bearing." This was also a great help when it came to familiarising myself with the main roads. These were vital knowledge, so that anytime there was a high-risk job, or something that required an immediate response, you could know from your current location what the fastest route to travel was. This was often achieved by sticking to the main roads or using them as bearings. In regard to the main roads, another colleague explained them so simply; I kicked myself for not picking up on it. He named a couple of the main roads we always used, and said these ones travel east to west, and then a couple of others that travelled north to south. They're your primary markers through the whole district, work off them as your central reference points, and everything else will fall into place.

I was quickly appreciating that Holden Hill was exposing me to some very important skill sets, vital to the success of a police officer. However, when looking for trouble is a big part of your profession, just like Hindley Street, I was being exposed to the extremes of human emotions, the traumatic turmoil of psychological damage and the devastating impact of alcohol and substance abuse from our local population. On Hindley Street, we spent a lot of time at the hospital, or at least visiting the hospital on a regular basis. One such incident that took place at the Modbury Hospital, would be one that unexpectedly stayed with me for a while. Mainly for the reason that my colleague was exposed in the worse way an officer can be, with potential life altering impacts if the outcome is severe; that exposure was too an offender's blood.

Chapter Ten

"A commitment to this service means facing some frightening realities."

Police are exposed to risks every day. It comes with the job when you've sworn to uphold the law and serve the community by protecting it from evil and even itself. Within their community, police are often immersed in its underbelly. There's the surface of how that community functions and appears. To most civilians, everyone is living out their lives, preoccupied with their own personal agendas and going through their daily patterns completely undisturbed by the darkness and chaotic turmoil that is always lurking beneath the surface. Most of the time, the very existence of this otherworld is entirely removed from their conscious thoughts, and until it comes crashing into their path, and disturbing their world, it will remain unseen and unthought of to them. Their home, and the surrounding areas that they're accustomed to seeing through a pleasant, familiar lens feels safe and secure to them. Perhaps on a subconscious level, it feels safe because it is familiar and predictable to them, and this instils a warm sense of security. Often when police are called, this security and predictability has been completely shattered and maybe for the first time in their lives, the chaos and intensity of another world that never sleeps has reared its ugly head for them to see.

This is the world that police are forever present in, and without their constant heroic and selfless actions, this world would explode into total anarchy, eating itself from within and spiralling out into the civilised world in a frenzy of trauma, aggression, and irrationality, with total disregard for the innocence its toxifying. This would often be a fascinating observation for me. It was something that came to my attention when I would finish a Saturday nightshift on Hindley Street, or really any especially intense nightshift on Hindley, and I would change into my civilian clothes, and walk down Hindley, sometimes to a nearby café for breakfast. So often, it would feel like coming out of a movie. You've just been caught up in a frenzied eight hours of fights, violence, substance overdoses, emotional intensity, and then at the end of your shift, if it has been a very busy shift, walking out of the station back into the street that just moments before were a storm of sirens, yelling and screaming, and now, it appears unnervingly normal and civilised as the crowds of people entering the city to start their working day are lining the streets. As I would walk amongst them, making eye contact with everyone I'd pass, sometimes I felt that the look on my face offered them a flash of a reflection from the world I have just departed from. It was always a surreal feeling, to see people arriving in the city early in the morning, when the chaos and disorder of the night has calmed, and the city comes back to life. People walking around in their suits, or fitness gear with an almost stern, blank look on their face as they are self-absorbed with their own thoughts and objectives for their day ahead, or whatever may be happening in their life. I almost felt a connection to all of them that everything I had just been through; they could somehow sense resonating from me and there was an unspoken recognition. Yet, I would know that looking into their eyes. There's every possibility they couldn't believe anything I would tell them from what myself, and my colleagues experienced when they were home safe sleeping soundly in their beds.

Sometimes in these moments, I'd feel a surreal detachment from the normality of the reality around me. Looking into the eyes of people who were just arriving into the city for work, my face perhaps reflecting all the chaos, aggression, mental health and intensity from the night before and something in my eyes staring into others to say they just don't know and can't understand what a journey into the abyss feels like.

A reality of the role, that never really made me flinch or have any real concerns or fears about, until later when I was truly questioning my place in the service, was the high degree of exposure police have to harmful diseases, through cross-contamination with bodily fluids like saliva, faeces, or blood. It's not uncommon for police to be spat on or be exposed to blood when someone has an open injury or there's been a violent incident. Back to the underbelly I was speaking about before, many characters who are always on the wrong side of the law have often been born into a world where crime to survive are simply a necessity. Whether it's born into poverty, or a lower-socioeconomic culture where life lessons to equip a young person to grow into a productive, independent and healthy person, who can positively contribute to society, are simply not held in high regard. This could be through the family dynamic or absence of one. Mental health, in many cases heightened by excessive alcoholism and drug-use also contributes to some of these characters inabilities to live a fulfilling independent life. Those basic fundamentals that are bred into many of us at such a young age, such as our health and hygiene, are not considered a priority for someone who has fallen down one of life's darker paths or has been born into chaos and poverty all together, with no guidance to discover their own awareness and practice of self-empowering traits such as resilience and self-belief. It would not be uncommon to encounter people known to have multiple mental health disorders, prone to violence and diagnosed with severe transmittable diseases including hepatitis. As there are no limitations to how deeply immersed police can go into these peoples' lives and personal space. A couple of stories on this topic, one that was particularly violent, stands out in my mind.

My field tutor and I had been tasked to a domestic disturbance at the main bus terminal in the area. When we arrived, there was a young male and female who appeared to be having a verbal argument. The female looked distressed and concerned, but the male appeared to be agitated and semi-confrontational. He also had an injury to his head, as there were spatters of blood on his face and arms. My partner has taken the male aside to try and speak to him, and I have turned my attention to the female. I realised quickly that she was just concerned for her friend, and while she was hesitant in talking initially, I showed I generally was empathetic and the reason I wanted to speak to her was so we could resolve the situation and offer her friend some support. Sometimes, in these interactions, people see the police uniform and automatically go on the defence, assuming police don't generally care about their situation, and that police won't be interested in actually listening to any grievances but will just take action and lock someone up. I've seen this reaction from people many times before, whether they've had constant dealings with police or perhaps a few bad experiences. I learnt very quickly, depending on the situation of course, if you could recognise someone's distress was out of concern or fear for another, showing them empathy and patience can instil in them an instant feeling of support, maybe even trust. Once they're over the initial resistance and hesitation of seeing the uniform, and realise there's a human being wearing the blue, through their distress, their perception can instantly change, and they start cooperating with you and talking to you. This was the case with this female. She was standoffish and all her attention was directed to her friend, but once she sensed something in me, perhaps that my intentions were genuinely what I was describing to her, there was an instant shift, and she began opening up to me and sharing more information like her name and what her concerns were for her friend.

I learnt that recently he had gotten very intoxicated and had injured himself pretty seriously. He had been drinking heavily for a long time since, from memory his father had suicided, and his brother was not in a good place too. So basically, this guy was in a mentally and emotionally unstable place and was showing signs of self-harm and self-destructive behaviour. He had some fresh-looking cuts around his neck, and we learned he had, only recently, tried to cut his neck. He had been drinking on this day and with us now there, his behaviour was becoming increasingly agitated and passive aggressive.

My partner and I were able to get through to him, to some degree and he sat on the bench, while my partner continued speaking with him. All the signs were there to justify to us that we should detain him under the Mental Health Act. He had visible signs of recent attempts to self-harm, especially around the neck which is a highly vulnerable place and lethal if cut in the wrong way. We were aware he was under severe emotional strain with the recent suicide of his father and other family conflicts. His friend, who said she had been with him for the last couple days, and that he'd basically been drinking consistently for that time, was witness to his erratic and self-destructive behaviour. Considering all these serious signs, we could determine he was unstable and a potential risk to himself or others. Under our authority, if we deem it reasonable, we can detain someone against their will, and take them into our care and custody and see that they receive a psychological assessment at the hospital. Of course, getting them on side and wanting to go to the hospital with us is always a mutually beneficial win for everyone. We're not detaining them because they've committed an offence, but we're actually protecting them from themselves and their own damaged and unpredictable state of mind. Often, this is against their will as they are already in a frenzied, confused, and confrontational state and, let's be honest, when you're saying you're fine and just leave me alone, and people you don't know are telling you otherwise and trying to force you to go somewhere you don't want too, that's probably going to piss off anyone in a sane state. This, of course, was a more severe and dangerous scenario, as the male was showing recent psychological and physical signs of being unstable, emotionally stressed from traumas in his life and erratic and impulsive behaviour. Basically, we were now invested, and our responsibility was to ensure he was cared for.

We convinced the male to come with us to the nearby hospital. His female friend could meet us there. Upon arriving, his behaviour began to escalate again. I'm not sure if it was because there was a lot of people in the waiting room, and he decided to glorify the fact that he was in police company. I had to encourage him to stay seated and reminded him of his language in the presence of other people, some of them children. We escorted him into another area of the hospital, where he laid down on a bed so nurses could speak to him and conduct their tests. Making assessments from the male's injury, his behaviour, his mental instability, and the information we gave them, the staff decided he would be staying overnight. Once this decision was shared with him, the situation quickly began to slip. He was adamant he wasn't staying, and the more this decision was explained to him, the more he decided he didn't want to be there altogether. He got out of his bed and went over to a nearby sink in his section for some water. I was facing him, talking to him, and trying to convince him this was the best place he could be right now for the state he was in. What I wasn't aware of, was hospital staff must have already called a code black. In a hospital, a code black is called when a patient becomes angry and potentially violent, is not being compliant and is not permitted to leave the hospital. This alarm basically sends as many security personnel as possible to that location. As I was talking to the male, trying to persuade him to relax and get back into his bed, what I didn't realise was behind me, a small army of security staff were gathering. This sight seemed to fuel the male, as he took on a wide stance with his arms outstretched, in a confrontational manner. Maybe beneath his bravado, he knew taking on two police officers and over five security staff was never going to work out for him, and he did return to his bed. But, once he did, perhaps knowing he was now in a position where he couldn't be taken down, but could still make the situation very difficult, he took the opportunity to kick up a scene. He refused to let any of the nurses near him and began thrashing and swiping at anything in reach. By this time, his female friend was there watching over, and still very concerned and heightened in her own way. At one point, she came over to the bed to be by his side, but still being emotional herself, she was getting him worked up and I eventually had to bear hug her, pick her up and carry her out of the cubicle where she could stand with nurses, and remain out of the way. Both my partner and I were either side of his bed, I remember at one point he grabbed my shirt sleeve up around my shoulder, squeezing it. Security staff all took up positions around the bed. I ended up putting his right foot into an ankle lock, and pretty much anywhere there was room for someone to get their hands on him and control him, they did. During the frenzy, and with my attention on his leg and foot, what I didn't see was his original injury to his head had reopened, and blood was pouring down his face. To make matters worse, he began spitting and spraying blood everywhere through his spluttering, making things as difficult as possible for everyone around him. My partner's face was near the male's head at this time and got a face full of splattered blood sprayed into him. Eventually, the male was subdued, I think by a sedative from hospital staff that put him to sleep.

My partner and I hung around at the hospital so he could do a series of tests, to determine if he was either clear or infected with something as a result of the exposure to the male's blood. What I noticed quickly was that my partner, an experienced officer, was not emotional in the slightest. He didn't appear to be overly stressed or anxious about this situation. Whether this was his experience and knowledge in managing these types of risks playing a part, or perhaps he was suppressing some of his own concerns to also assist me, in keeping me calm and to disregard the level of concern and stress in the moment. Early the next day, he received confirmation from his doctor that there was no contamination or infections, that was a huge sigh of relief for me and I'm sure a massive one for him and his family. Until those results come back, you cannot have close contact with loved ones, as you may now be infected with a serious transferrable disease. I've heard stories of officers whose lives have drastically changed forever because they have been exposed to infectious diseases through contamination.

As relieved as I was for my colleague, it suddenly put a new layer of concern in my mind for the very real, and long-term risks associated with this role. Previously, I had never carried any concerns, in fact I completely disregarded any sense of self-preservation in answering the call to service. I had thought about the risk of potential injury in the line of duty, but just thought that is something I can recover from and it's a small price to pay to ensure justice and that I am upholding my sworn oath to the very best of my ability and commitment. I had never considered the risk of exposure to transmittable diseases, and the forever-altering impact it could have.

Only a few months into my probation, I had met a woman whose impact on me caused me to fall deeply in love with her, finding that limitless connection in another who I can proudly say is my soulmate and partner in life. Thankfully, she felt the same way about me. At the time of this incident, our relationship with each other was full of so much natural love, passion, expression, communication, openness, and inspiration that it felt effortless. After this incident, and I was waiting in the hospital with my colleague, thoughts were flashing through my mind of the love I had for my partner and the limitless feeling of freedom that we shared in our connection together, and how it would feel if our affection and expression towards one another had to be limited. How I would feel going home having to have that conversation if I was infected with a long-term or even forever transmittable disease. I couldn't even fathom just the thought of such a thing happening, and I began to have my own doubts as to how far my commitment would really carry me in this career.

Certain taskings we'd respond too would present this risk of exposure to blood, or other bodily excrements much more than others. Just the very nature of the tasking, gathered from the information sent to us as we were making our way there alerted you to the fact that this situation you were about to enter, and this person you're about to deal with could put you, your colleague, and everyone else involved at great risk.

On another occasion, I was on patrol with my same field tutor as the hospital incident. The details of the tasking we received were as follows. The call had come in from a social worker, who was a carer for a young man living with an intellectual disability. While the man lived independently, he had carers who would regularly be over at the house, or who would live onsite close by. Apparently, this male had an obsession with finding syringes, anywhere on the ground and using them to self-harm and stab and cut himself. On this occasion, the carer was concerned as he had heard the male returned to the house during the night, and he felt that he had syringes on him or had hidden them somewhere in the house, knowing they would be confiscated. This was a huge concern if he had hidden them, as it meant he could harm himself at any time or the needles could harm carers as they moved about the house while cleaning up.

We arrived and were greeted by the carer who called us, and the carer who was currently on shift. We received further information regarding the situation. Apparently, a house on the same street was a known drug house, where people would frequent regularly, and this male had found discarded needles on the street and used them for his own obsessions. Plus, only a week or two earlier, when the male, who was prone to violent and emotional outbursts was having an episode, he had used a syringe to draw blood from himself and then spray it all over the walls inside his house. You can imagine some of the risk factors that we were establishing after hearing all of this. A male with an intellectual disability who has regular emotional and physical outbursts, has an obsession for finding needles wherever he can and using them on himself, and the fact that these are probably used and dirty needles so he could be infected, and a carrier of God knows what. From the outside looking in, it really was a sad story, but it was important in my mind to put the welfare of this male to the forefront of my thinking and decisions. I had to realise in this moment, I could be a part of a solution to protect a young person who was deeply depressed and without the psychological capacity to regulate his own behaviour and ways of thinking. Those who cared for him were now calling on us to assist, and once a situation has escalated enough to require police intervention, then it's serious.

Being made aware of this male's potential to unexpectedly become angry and violent, I felt it best if the carers' continued to communicate with him, and I would remain close by. These were people he knew and trusted, and it was when he felt judged or accused of something that would cause him to feel overwhelmed and then lash out. When he came out, he was a big boy. He had to be at least six foot four, or taller and had a build similar to the shape of Shrek. I don't mean that as any kind of insult, it was just my first initial observation, and the resemblance was uncanny. I realised that if he lost it, with his size and mental capacity, he would not act with any self-restraint or awareness as to just how big and strong he could be. As always, I was prepared to escalate above and beyond whatever was necessary to control the situation but looking at this male, I realised it would take some effort if I had to restrain him. I found I always felt a sense of preparedness and confidence if I visualised what actions I would do if the situation became physical. My training in self-defence was a huge advantage in these moments, as I could see in my mind how I could most efficiently, and safely take someone down and restrain them. What angle would I approach them, how would I get into an advantageous position behind them, how would I secure my arms around them to efficiently get them to the floor, while also minimising the risk of them hitting their head on the way down. All my training had prepared me with this knowledge, and while so often I never had to put it into practice, I felt mentally and physically prepared with what I had to do. That itself would already be a huge advantage over another, who may be acting from rage, or anger or a frenzied and uncontrolled state of mind. Compared to me who would be very clear and calculated in my actions.

I could see from the outset that this young man was already agitated, possibly with the number of people all at the property, two of his carers and a couple of police officers. The carer who had called police was talking with the male, trying to coerce him into giving up the needles. Initially, the male was hesitant and standoffish, just pacing around and not looking at anyone. He then led us on a small walk down the footpath to a nearby park, claiming he had dropped the needles somewhere in this area. His behaviour indicated to me he knew the needles weren't here and he was just leading us astray. We eventually made our way back to the house and went inside. The carer and I stayed with the male, while others looked around the house. His intellectual disability seemed severe, having the behaviours and articulation of perhaps a young child, despite the fact he was about 16 years old. We could all see his behaviour becoming more tense and agitated, pacing around, keeping his head down and avoiding certain questions.

The male, his carer and I all ended up outside, in the back area of the house and the garage. Somehow, we had established the needles were hidden in old cans that were in recycling bags, but as the carer put more pressure on the male and questioned him about this, the male diverted more and mumbled some things that implied he did not like being accused on things he hadn't done. The carer leant over to me and whispered this is what happened a week or two prior when the male had sprayed blood all around the house. His behaviour indicated he was reaching that same level of frustration. In preparation for him to turn physical or violent, I subtlety unclipped my taser holster, just in case I had to draw it. However, the carer was excellent in his negotiations. The male had said he wanted to find the needles, but it was everyone distrusting him and not letting him out of our sight that was agitating him. To show him some good faith and trust, we agreed to stand on the other side of the gate, giving him the chance to go through the recycling bags and present the needles without us watching over his every move. The carer and I both agreed, while there was an element of risk, as we were leaving the male alone, and if he wanted he could have found a needle and done whatever he wanted, we thought we would give him the benefit of the doubt, show we can trust him and give him the opportunity to do the right thing.

We stood on the other side of the gate, listening to plastic bags being rummaged through and rubbish being scattered. When we re-entered, I had my right-hand hovering near my taser in case he pulled something on us or changed his mind, didn't want to cooperate and became violent. Thankfully, he presented a small number of needles and sheepishly handed them over to the carer.

Upon reflection, I was proud of myself with how I performed throughout the situation, and most of all, being an active part of the solution that resulted in the best possible outcome for everyone. Considering a similar scenario had occurred only a week or two earlier, with a very different outcome, that being blood sprayed all over the walls. This was as peaceful an outcome as the carers could have hoped for. The carer who was with me at the end, thanked me, just as I commended him for his ability to connect with the male and establish understanding and trust. Some of the most rewarding parts of this job were these moments, when the anticipated storm has past, the dust has settled and the outcome no one expected, that being a peaceful, positive and nonconfrontational one, has been achieved. To have someone involved in the moment thank you for your service, or even to send in an acknowledgment of your actions and attitude, the motivation that would surge in me was full of gratitude. Because in a crisis situation, your presence, professionalism, composure, and awareness have all contributed to the most beneficial outcome possible, and in policing, any situation that is resolved peacefully, or with mutual cooperation is as big a win as you could ever hope for.

In this situation, my colleague had taken more of a backseat role and allowed me to take the lead and manage the incident. I was expecting it to erupt at any moment, I mean all the warning signs were there, the male's behaviour and what had previously happened in a very similar scenario. So, knowing I could communicate with a vulnerable person, establish enough trust, and exude a presence that kept them calm, while also controlling the momentum of the incident to reach a peaceful resolution, I allowed myself the small feeling of victory to fill me with confidence and propel me forward.

In the end, after he had handed over the needles, two paramedics had arrived on scene and tried to talk to him. The one speaking was exceptional in her ability to connect and seek cooperation, as most paramedics I worked alongside were. They often had a very calming and caring influence, while knowingly guiding the person to make decisions that were in their favour and would allow the paramedics to execute their duties. The male reluctantly agreed to get into the ambulance. I rode along in the back as a safety escort, as was standard when conveying a potentially aggressive or violent person to hospital.

As I'm sharing these stories, so much of the details come flooding back to me as I recall them, but what isn't clear is the date they occurred. So, while I feel like sharing these stories flows in some type of synchronicity, that's more so from a theme or a realisation that they fit into, and not any type of chronological order.

Chapter Eleven

"Maybe you don't expect it, but these things can stay with you."

I was almost three years with the South Australia Police. My first 12 months as a cadet training at the Academy, which as I've shared is an entirely all-consuming roller coaster of a year. Then, almost two years on probation, where from day one, you're literally exposed to everything on the job, regardless of your experience and preparedness. You're about to get your hands dirty in the most challenging, fulfilling and diverse career in the world. If I think hard enough, I feel like I can recall almost every incident, tasking and interaction I would have ever been a part of. Maybe this is an exaggeration, but so much of the emotions, my thought processes, feelings both mentally and physically in the present moment are as clear in my mind now as the moment they happened. When I think of some of the things I did, and saw and was a part of, I am suddenly teleported back to that very moment in my mind, where so much of what occurred I can relive in vivid detail. That's what really inspired me to begin writing this. Once I started, I realised how therapeutic it felt and how much I was enjoying taking all my thoughts, feelings and realisations conjured up from my time in an intense working environment and exploring them in my own words. By doing this, I've been able to arrive to new depths of understanding and appreciation for my experiences as a police officer and sharing them with an array of remarkable and heroic people who show up every day, ready to commit everything to protecting their community. Plus, by doing this I've realised there are a few moments during my career that really rise to the surface amongst the rest. This one comes to mind for a number of reasons. It was the first time I was driving during a large-scale high-speed pursuit, during which I came within just seconds, and only a few short metres from having a head-on collision, a close call that is still burnt in my memory.

My team were on nightshifts, which for us meant seven consecutive shifts of working 11:00 p.m. until about 7:30 a.m. For this week, you were basically living in a parallel dimension, one where time and total cognitive functioning could feel like illusions. For me, usually getting into the middle of the week was when the impact of working nights was taking full affect. Having to sleep during the day, waking up regularly and eventually waking up completely disoriented as to what time it actually was. Often getting to sleep was easy, and sometimes I could barely remember getting from the couch to bed. Usually enjoying some down time, putting a movie on, having a decent feed and a glass of shiraz would do the trick. Before I ever started nightshifts, the thought of having alcohol at around eight or nine in the morning I never would have imagined even in my wildest temptations. However, nightshift is a completely different beast all together and after working an eight-hour shift, sometimes they'd be the busiest shifts of the roster, having a sneaky swig was a welcomed warm blanket waiting for you at home. Functioning throughout this week was, while never difficult, it was a surreal feeling. I'd describe it as never feeling fully awake, while never feeling like you could completely full asleep. It was some blurry spaced-out state of being somewhere in the middle. I even remember when I was still on Hindley Street, I was doing a CrossFit class at about 7:15 p.m., at the time I was living in a town house with a friend in the Adelaide CBD, and our CrossFit gym was on the same street, paradise! I was working that night at 11:00 p.m. and was already a few shifts into the week. The workout had hand-release push-ups and I was having micro-naps each time I'd lay flat on the floor. People who sleepwalk would have felt more awake than me at the time.

But anyway, back to the story. My colleague and I were patrolling the streets, I was driving. Whether he had switched radio channels to another district, or had been made aware somehow, my colleague heard of a pursuit currently happening. It involved one suspect vehicle, and multiple police vehicles. Originally, I think it was a suspect trying to break into houses, or he had already been on a crime spree and was now leading police all over the Western District. This covered some of the major coastal suburbs such as Port Adelaide, Henley Beach, and Glenelg. From the information being received, the vehicle was making its way towards the city, or at least the streets that ran parallel with the city. Just on the outskirts of the city, we positioned ourselves strategically in anticipation of intercepting the vehicle if it came our way.

We positioned ourselves on a road island at a major intersection. Being the early hours of the morning, traffic was pretty much non-existent. These early hours were often a ghost town when patrolling the suburbs. My colleague and I were listening in to the regular updates over the radio, while he was simultaneously checking the road maps, trying to anticipate the direction of the suspect vehicle, and where the most advantageous routes would be for us to join the pursuit, or potential locations that we could move to intercept and set up road spikes.

From the information we were receiving, this was an escalating situation. There were at least five or more police vehicles involved, plus Pol-Air were providing support. Pol-Air is the police helicopter, and a huge resource when trying to locate a suspect over a large area, or in this case, be able to provide regular updates as to the direction and manner of driving of a suspect vehicle. Even if police vehicles lose sight of it, Pol-Air have the advantage of being able to maintain visual and direct police as to the location and direction of the vehicle, or the suspect if they decide to dump the vehicle and run.

Reports were coming in that the vehicle had rammed a number of police vehicles in this pursuit, so clearly this was a high-risk situation with a dangerous and desperate offender driving a weapon that needed to get shutdown immediately. It was around this point that my partner decided we had to join the pursuit; the more police involved the greater the chance of stopping the suspect sooner.

I took off assertively in the direction that the suspect was reported, my colleague was constantly moving around the map as frequent updates were coming in as to the vehicle's direction. As we got closer, we got an idea of just how many police vehicles were involved, as it didn't matter what main road or dark side street you'd travel down, there seemed to be sirens everywhere and police moving in every direction. This was a full-scale pursuit.

It was my first time driving during a major pursuit like this, so I did my best to listen in on the radio for updates, but I put my full attention into my driving. My very experienced colleague was multi-tasking like a pro, listening to the radio and using that to map our best course. These skills come with experience. It's a blend of knowing your policing district and its suburbs and streets, having an experienced ear that can instinctively hear information as it comes in, while using that to navigate and intercept. During a crisis response, there is a lot happening, but for those who have been in the job for years, it's like someone who has been training and mastering a physical skill, it's a skillset that with practice becomes second nature, instinctive. This was a reminder to me of my inexperience and how much I had to learn, but what I could do efficiently in this moment was drive and drive well. My colleague, who was a field tutor I had probably worked with the most during my time in Holden Hill, knew this about me and he specified with very clear instructions how I should drive, based on the updates coming in. If he said 'cruise', I would just coast along at a slow speed, if he said 'stop' I would in our tracks, and if he said 'floor it' or some variation, it didn't matter if we were down a dark and sleepy single lane side street or a multilane main road, I would gun it. Usually if police were responding to an urgent task, the guideline would usually be to exceed the speed limit by about twenty kilometres. That's with lights and sirens going. If you just had to move through traffic, but no lights and sirens, maybe ten kilometres. Naturally, as the speed goes up, the risk goes up with it. In this situation, the most important thing was getting to a particular location fast, ahead of the pursuit, so there weren't always restraints in how fast we were going to get there.

A couple times, we positioned ourselves to lay down road spikes, but then the direction of the vehicle would change again, and we'd be back on the move. Most of the time, I never even saw the suspect vehicle, and with so many police vehicles moving around the area in the same manner as us, sometimes the risk was getting around them as they were reversing or anticipating where they were going.

We found ourselves driving down a dark side street, amongst some industrial buildings. There wasn't any street lighting, and we were moving at speed knowing the suspect vehicle was close by in the area. We drove over a small intersection where another police vehicle was stationary. Suddenly ahead of us, on the same street we were and coming directly towards us I saw the silhouette of a moving vehicle. It didn't have any headlights on, so I immediately thought it was one of ours, moving around covertly with no lights. All I could see was its silhouette illuminated against the dark night sky, but I quickly noticed the manner it was driving. It was snaking all over the road, side to side and I realised this wasn't a police vehicle, police wouldn't drive that recklessly. It suddenly dawned on me this was the suspect, and I had unknowingly ended up in a game of chicken with him. I instinctively yelled out, "Fuck!" and slammed the brakes on. Seconds before I did, the vehicle threw its high-beam headlights on, and as we braked, the vehicle broke as well, bunny hoping around us until it was on my side and then it floored it back in the direction we'd just come. The police vehicle we had just past continued after it. I slammed us into reverse, turned around and recommenced the pursuit. In this moment, there wasn't any time to process exactly what had just happened, or how close we had just come to colliding head-on with a vehicle at high-speed. Our vehicle had been stationary for only a few seconds, and when the suspect broke and threw his lights on, he was so close to us that when the nose of his vehicle tilted towards the ground from the sudden change in momentum, his headlights disappeared beneath the view of our front bonnet.

We re-joined the pursuit, which took us all the way back close to the city and along some of the major roads surrounding the area. I was able to get a better look at the suspect vehicle, which appeared to be similar to a Land Rover. He was doing some unusual things, besides ramming police vehicles and trying to outrun police of course. When he was approaching a corner, he would put his hazard lights on. I don't know if this was a deterrent somehow or intended to be a distraction.

Eventually, I think the vehicle ran over some spikes and made it to Port Road, a major multilane road that runs along part of the perimeter outside the city. The vehicle had come to a stop and apparently the male suspect had gotten out and tried to run but was subdued in the middle of the road by officers who were close behind. We arrived just after he was taken down. My partner and I jumped out of our vehicle and hit the ground running, sprinting to assist the other officers. The suspect was already restrained on the ground, on his stomach and hands handcuffed behind his back. As was always instinctive for me, I found some space on the suspect that I could get my hands too and assist in restraining, not knowing if he was resisting and making life for the two officers very difficult. After so much time on Hindley Street, I had learnt you never assume officers have a suspect under control, and if they have their head and arms restrained, then I'm jumping on the legs. Until it's obvious that a suspect is restrained, handcuffed and not being difficult or violent, then you assume they're still a risk to themselves and others. Even on their stomach and handcuffed, suspects can spit or slam their heads into the ground. On Hindley Street, there was one occasion on a weekend nightshift where a young man was victim to the violent frenzied effects of a substance, most likely ice or acid. There were five of us all restraining him on the footpath, as he was gnarling and trying to bite anything that moved. We had to support his head as he was ramming it into the footpath, and even trying to bite the pavement. He was in a state where he had no physical or mental control over himself anymore, and whatever he had taken had turned him into a runaway train. Even with five of us on him, we were all working hard.

It took about forty minutes for paramedics to arrive, and for that entire time, we were all working hard to keep him both subdued and safe. With the state of mind he was in, his physicality was erratic, unpredictable and without restraint. Meaning his adrenal system was in a frenzy and his physical movements were exerted with relentless strength and power. I remember at one point; I was on his legs trying to get them into a leg lock. One of his legs was free and I leant my bodyweight down on it, trying to hook it into his other leg. At the time, I was probably around 90 kilograms, actually close to 100 with all our equipment to consider. With one leg, he drove me back until I was almost off balanced and thrown off him. That and needing five grown men to keep him down should say enough.

Back to the pursuit. Having experienced numerous encounters like this, I never took any chances when seeing officers restraining someone on the ground, and after everything this guy had just put us all through, I already knew we were dealing with a violent, dangerous unhinged human being. One of the officers backed away, so I replaced him, lowering to one knee by the suspect's side, and having one hand on his arm, and one hand on his temple, to keep his head sideways and pressed against the road. This was my go-to position for a couple of reasons, and none of them were ever to be malicious or to inflict pain just for the fun of it. By keeping a person's head restrained to the side, you minimise greatly their strength and ability to throw their head around. When a person is head on, or in a neutral position, the alignment of the spine to the cranium (aka the skull) and the way that joint works enables them to exert a lot more force in pushing the head back and force. Holding them in this side position greatly weakens the force that can be exerted through that joint. Especially against the ground, or a wall, I would always hold a person's head in this position if they were being difficult or resistant. My intentions for it always were, no matter what their behaviour was like or how they reacted, was for their safety, my colleagues and my own. I'd rather have them secured in this way, and calling me one of many affectionate names, than risk them smashing their head into something hard. A simple action that causes an injury like that, besides obviously the physical trauma and injury, it can cause a cascading effect of additional work and internal investigations into your management of the suspect and your safety procedures.

Back to our suspect. I could tell he was under the influence of some kind of substance, his arms were wet with perspiration, and he was rapid fire speed talking, half of it didn't make any sense. A couple of things he did say, "I was never going to hurt anyone," and he seemed pretty proud of his efforts to evade police. I respectfully reminded him that he was restrained in the middle of Port Road, in police custody, so his efforts to evade us weren't worth bragging about. A cage vehicle arrived, and he was loaded into the back, and taken away by the arresting team. Some shifts could be like this, they seem unnervingly quiet (by the way the 'Q' word is forbidden in conversation amongst police) and instantly a large-scale, coordinated job that attracts media cover erupts.

It wasn't until the end of that shift, when I could truly relax and finally take the cloak of constant hyper-vigilance and readiness off, that I began to reflect on the events of the night. From the time we were stationary on the traffic island ready to join the pursuit, to the moment the suspect was put in the back of the cage car, the entire experience lasted, from a vague memory over two hours. So much of it I had been in a surreal blended state of automatic actions, and intense concentration. In these dangerous moments, a skill like high-risk driving falls back to quality and consistency of your training. Thankfully, as we are driving every day, the fundamental driving skills are reinforced over and over, and when you're pushing the envelope further and driving at high speeds, changing direction suddenly, cornering at speed, and overall increasing the risk and increasing the consequences of error, those fundamentals are you and your partner's lifeline.

I found that the faster I was driving and the more that was demanded of me, the more natural and automatic these skills become. This was a similar experience to activating Flow State like I described back at Mallala during my driving test. Because of the heightened element of risk and danger, the greater my awareness and consciousness in my present state became. I was concentrating so intensely, very aware that lives, that of my own and my colleague, and anyone in the area, was solely reliant on my abilities and mental composure. This elevated state of connection with the present moment and your actions within it, naturalises all those hours of skill repetition, as you're no longer thinking just about them, or consciously aware you're doing them, but they're the many moving parts that enable you to perform at your peak state, to accomplish something greater or that can only be achieved by demanding the best within yourself and to arrive in that hyper-aware conscious place of performance.

This situation brought back echoes in my mind of a statement one of my driving instructors had said. It went something along the lines of, "Criminals will always drive at higher risk, reckless and take greater chances in an attempt to lose us or make it so dangerous that we terminate the pursuit. However, we will always be trained, and that will always be our advantage."

A realisation I had, that didn't fully sink in with me until much later after the night was over, was how close I had come to having a head-on high-speed collision with the suspect. Out of no fault of my own, my colleague and I were merely seconds away and one wrong (well, one more) wrong decision to be made by a suspect on a crime spree and juiced up to the eyeballs on a cocktail of substances. Reflecting on this, I found myself questioning a lot why he had even decided to avoid colliding with us all together. He had already proven earlier in the pursuit that he would be willing to do anything to get away, including colliding with police vehicles. As quickly and instinctively as that moment occurred, there was nothing I could have done to avoid a head-on. I had literally last second slammed on our brakes, but that did nothing to take us out of the path of collision. When the realisation sets in that you were milliseconds away from a major incident, where the likelihood of physical injury was high, but to what extent I have never thought too deeply into it. You still find yourself contemplating just how close it was and how devastating that split second could have become. Similarly to when I ran into the taxi that pulled out in front of me on Hindley Street. As quickly as the potential for the incident passed us by, so too did my concern for what the worst possible outcome could have been. In the heat of the moment, we were in response mode and just concerned about catching this guy. Even as he bunny-hopped around us that night, I was kicking myself that I hadn't swerve to ram him and box him in. This of course goes against any police procedures, and I would have been seriously reprimanded for those actions, the risk to human life taken and the deliberate damage to a police vehicle.

While this incident has echoed in my mind over and over, and at the most unexpected times or when something triggers it to remerge in my memory box, I've never been consumed with thoughts or anxieties or 'what if?' Meaning my thoughts running away from me and causing me anxiety with thoughts of the worst things that could have happened in that moment. If this was the case, I would be severely concerned, and realise that I have been traumatised from the event and in need of professional guidance. Actually, this is something I have contemplated on, why being involved in such an extreme situation, and coming so close to danger with a devastating result has not played more on my mind, in the present when it was happening and for some time after. At least, my understanding of it is my personal association with fear and risk of consequences. I've never been a nervous person; in fact I can never recall a time I felt nervous. Whether it's getting up and talking in front of people, performing in my Year 12 drama assessment in front of an audience, before a championship match when I played basketball, or any competition or any academic assessment. Nerves have never been an interfering factor for me. Now, having said that I have always been excited prior to these occasions, and as I've come to understand more over the years, this always came down to a few consistent elements and how I interpreted the feelings of anticipation.

I felt prepared. None of these occasions in my life, whether it was sporting or just to entertain, none of them I ever went into feeling any doubt in my ability to show-up in that moment or concerns over my preparation or the work I had put in prior to it. This pre-performance excitement stemmed from my enthusiasm to showcase something that I believed I had worked hard for and could impact others through displaying the results of consistent commitment and dedication to refining this craft.

Once you understand what makes something scary, fear becomes transparent, just like looking through a window. Initially, the essence of fear, that immediate feeling is like looking at that window with the curtains closed. You can't see clearly, you are uncertain about what lays on the other side because you can't see it, and with no seeing there's an inability to understand. Once you take the courageous step to draw those curtains back, choosing to face your fear, you have a greater sense of clarity about the source of that fear in you. You've already chosen to understand it, which immediately alleviates any hesitation, now that you're inviting it into your space. Through that window, with clarity you can see where that source of fear has been ignited from. It's the same when you see an angry person, or a person trying to be intimidating or dominating. Our fear comes from our uncertainty of how we will handle ourselves when confronted with that person. Or the primal survival instinct to avoid physical injury. When I saw this so often policing, it became humorous to me, as this person would be doing everything to stand over you, to bang their chest, gnarl their teeth and flex their muscles, while in my mind I'm thinking well, this person has no idea who I am, they have no idea of what my capabilities might be. So, to confront a complete unknown with an inflated ego, was already a weak point in their armour, as they're trying to assert dominance from a place of egotistical disguise, to mask their own hesitation and insecurity. Even more so, it was a desperate attempt to mask their own fear and uncertainty of just what they're dealing with, knowing full well that they have no idea and they're compensating by trying to take the initiative. Blindly charging themselves up with bravado and shallow courage.

This probably doesn't explain my lack of fear in the moment of almost being crushed head-on. Because it didn't happen, and really there wasn't any time to even think about being afraid before it happened, all I can draw on is my reflections on just how close that situation was from turning out very different. I've found through this example, and others that inspire reflection and contemplation, is they bring with them a wave of appreciation. In this moment, coming so close to something devastating, upon reflection instilled in me a greater sense of appreciation and inspired in me a greater desire to be grateful, for the love I have experienced in my life, the connections I'm lucky to share, my relationship with my family and my friends, and gratitude that the person I am aspiring to be in this world is motivated through service to others, to be a positive impact on others.

This practice of reflection, gratitude and appreciation became a constant mechanism for me, to protect myself mentally and emotionally from some of the traumas and confronting sights I'd see. When you would see how some people live, the agony on their minds and the squalor they exist in, I felt that the more I too invest myself into their world, driven by my professional obligations, then I had a responsibility to myself to equally and intentionally protect myself from falling victim to those traumas. Some things you can never unsee, however, with a clear perspective and an intentional mindset, you can allow the natural thoughts and shocks that come racing to your mind to not take control of it, and this does take effort and practice. Whether you want to live a healthy or unhealthy life, both of them take effort, both require the consistent practice of habits. I found in policing, the development and practice of emotional awareness, and emotional intelligence would be vital, a powerful armour in a police officer's arsenal. When you're being confronted and deeply immersing, pretty much on a daily basis, in emotional anarchy, trauma, violence, death, disorder, and abuse to children that has no limits (I could go on and on) being emotionally aware and checking-in with yourself constantly are vital strategies to enable yourself to navigate your way through that chaos, while maintaining your clarity in your own identity, being present in meaningful moments in life and actively practicing gratitude and appreciation, to remind yourself of what you're actually thankful for in life. When an officer forgets these things, or loses sight of even how to be thankful, because their world is jaded by the debilitating and dark levels of energy that they exist in for so much of their life. When these lines of morality are blurred behind thick clouds of black smoke, a person's entire outlook on the world, and on humanity will only reflect that thick darkness, which can cause every other facet of their life to suffer, whether they're becoming distant or reactive with loved ones and friends as their mind is so clouded by the frenzied trauma of every job they've attended. Without that emotional preparedness and self-management, a person's mind can be easily fractured and manipulated, toxified from the inside out, and gradually day after day, shift after shift, their entire perception of who they are, and the world they exist can be stained, like breathing smoke for the rest of your life and feeling your inner health gradually deteriorating. Some officers I saw first-hand and spoke too, years and years of experience had a deeply far-gone jaded and resentful outlook on the world, life and seemingly everything in it. Even when you'd share some of a perspective that you know carries uplifting and inspirational connotations, their response would be one of rejection, or somehow finding a way to smother it with shit and degradation. After talking to them long enough, or just observing their general attitude and the nature and energy they would bring into their interactions, I'd be thinking to myself, *Their entire outlook would inhibit them from ever truly enjoying anything in life.* How can you move forward in your life with true momentum, when every step you're taking feels like you're dragging your feet through the mud? How can you ever be grateful, when all your energy and effort is then focused on complaining about the mud on your shoes?

I was seeing and learning a lot every day on the job. More and more I was discovering about myself and certain reactions I was having in response to what I was being exposed too. So often, I would feel proud about how I showed up in the moment. How I instinctively reacted in the face of danger, or, as my skills developed, how automatic some of my thought processes and decision making was becoming. There was naturally a darker side to this evolution, one I was becoming aware of the more time I spent in this world. I began to feel a sense of my compassion and empathy towards humanity shift at times. No matter what a person's current emotional state was, or what else was happening around me, I knew deep down if I had to use force, I could trigger that side in me with relentless and bare rawness, almost numbing emotional sensation in the face of extreme violence. I began to wonder, if I stared down into that psychological abyss within me, who or what would I become if I chose to leap into it.

Chapter Twelve

"I've got you in my sights."

Firearms training was one of the other highlights for me as a cadet. It was a one-week course at the Academy, where they have their own firing range. Half my course-mates did the training at the beginning of Phase Two, while the rest of us spent our time on Out Phase, and then we'd swap over. We were trained to proficiency in the standard issue sidearm of the police, what we would carry every day on patrols. Everything from start-of-shift and end-of-shift procedures, which is basically a safety routine to ensure the firearm is not loaded, and fully functional for operation…"Point safe – check safe – remove magazine – tilt – cock – lock – look, chamber, magwell, breach face – Feel, chamber, magwell, breach face – weapon clear!"

We learnt how to take apart and reassemble the firearm, memorising all the key working parts. How to deal with stoppages, firing from varying distances, speed drills, double-taps, and firearm scenarios. At the end of the week, we were put through a series of firing assessments that would determine your percentage of competency. I really enjoyed the skillsets to handle and operate a firearm with efficiency. When you can draw your weapon from its holster and fire with accuracy, all done with speed and efficiency and so naturally that it's simply reflex, you feel a level of professional capacity that just can't come without training such unique skills. This was a skill that with repetition, I quickly developed a level of above average efficiency, at least in a controlled environment in the firing range. When it came to our assessments at the end of the course, over the seven (that's a vague estimate) shooting scenarios, I was one round off getting 100%, and that round was my own fault of thinking I had fired all the rounds I needed to for that scenario, when I actually missed one. Otherwise, all my rounds were on target.

In my nearly two years on probation, I only ever drew my firearm on one occasion. But, before your imagination starts to run too wild, it was to terminate an injured kangaroo, which, as like so much of my other encounters in uniform, has an entire story behind it.

The only time I came close to drawing my firearm on another person was in a stand-off between a crazed male and police. It started with a typical traffic stop, and then the male driver running from police, yelling he has a gun and will kill any cops who come near him. As you can imagine, a call like that gets a lot of attention.

I think we were on nights. The traffic stop was only a short distance from Holden Hill Police Station, and when we got the call over the radio, of a male, possibly with a firearm has just run from police threatening to kill them, the speed of everything you do, from kitting up to getting to our fleet, everything is accelerated. It's amazing how in moments like this, when there's a serious incident on, police will kick it up a gear from cruise control to full throttle in an instant, and all the training and responsiveness kicks into high gear.

My colleague and I motored down the main road to the location of the original traffic stop. The male had reportedly run into a nearby suburb, and they had lost sight of him amongst the darkened houses and streets. When we pulled up, there was already a heavy police presence of vehicles and officers moving in every direction. With reports of a firearm, we put our vests on before going by foot into the suburban area. It was communicated to me to move down the road and set up a stationary cordon. There was already a lot of officers moving throughout the area searching for this guy, down the side-lanes of houses and all over the street. As I was moving down the road, a probie on my team, junior to me had just arrived and asked what she should do, I suggested the first thing is to vest up, before getting into any position.

Another officer, one I recognised from the Academy, was already in the middle of the road. I took up a similar position to her but keeping a distance between us to stay spaced a part. With searches like this, it's like fishing with a net. police will establish the last known location of the suspect, and then cast a large net, setting up outer and inner perimeters, and then gradually as the search continues, the idea is to trap the suspect in and tighten the net, so they have no way to slip through.

The suspect was located on top of a house roof. Cordons were being set up all over the place and an officer, one of my field tutors had established communication with the suspect. Over the radio, I could hear updates of all different departments as to their status. Firefighters, Paramedics, SAPOL

Negotiators and Special Tasks and Rescue (STAR Force). Firefighters were on standby, as they have ladders to get access to a roof. Paramedics would remain in the area, but for their safety, they would not move in closer until the threat and danger of the situation was all clear. STAR Force, South Australia's SWAT, were enroute to the scene, but could not be there for an extended time. Negotiators arrived and remained close by, since my colleague had already established a degree of rapport and communication with the suspect.

The entire time, officers had a visual of the suspect, they were trying to confirm if there was a firearm in the male's possession. Where I was standing, still in the middle of the road, I couldn't see the suspect, however, I rotated with another officer who was standing in the backyard of a house, so he could get a vest. The backyard was very dark, with some tree coverage. It was also on a slope, and the roof where the suspect was standing on was further down the hill, off to the side about 20–30 metres away. I made sure I turned off any light emitting equipment I was carrying. I could see the suspect over the top of the backyard fence, but I was in complete darkness, so any light I would project, such as lights on my camera or my torch would be like a fluorescent spotlight illuminating exactly where I was to the suspect. Cover of darkness were my greatest concealment, and the suspect never would have had any idea that I was watching his every move.

My eyes remained on him like a hawk, watching his every move and observing his demeanour and emotional stress. I could hear some of his yelling, and he basically sounded like a guy who was at the end of his rope and couldn't see any reason for him to be existing in this world anymore. He said a couple of times if police made attempts to get on the roof, he would start shooting, but I never saw anything that resembled a firearm. He was stating very clearly that he wasn't going to come quietly, and he wanted to get shot by STAR just to end it all. When you're hearing a person make these claims, and they've already gone so far as to threaten to kill police. In my mind, I was preparing myself that the only way this was coming to a conclusion was through a violent act, whether that was a shootout or this male ending his own life. From his demeanour, his refusal to comply with any requests from police and the threats he was making, we were in for a long night.

I remember so clearly the thought processes I was going through during this night. I was in a situation where I was facing a desperate man, who had made violent threats to my colleagues and had basically stated that STAR would have to shoot him to get him off the roof. Put all those elements together, and you have a volatile mix of responsibility and retribution. I tried to remain empathetic towards him, and still seeing him as a human being, just one who had failed within himself to practice the resilience and perseverance to overcome some of life's tests. However, if that self-defeating attitude and resentment towards everything that's gone wrong in his life, takes him so far that he is willing to hurt, or threaten to hurt my brothers and sisters in blue, or any innocent people, I would not have a moment of hesitation in taking him down.

These thoughts, among many others were flooding through my head. My right hand felt light and fast, anticipating at any second the reflexive action of reaching for my firearm, drawing it, and getting this guy dead in my sights. The entire time I was watching him, I was playing out the scenario in my mind of what the situation would become, if he pulled out a firearm and began shooting. I knew, with how prepared and focused I was, that my firearm would be out in a flash, taking aim before I have even felt the movement of my hand (training and repetition has that effect) especially when you know that your ability to execute that responsibility is potentially a life-or-death situation.

From the position I was standing, and the distance I was from the suspect, while it was about 20–30 metres, I felt that I could be on target to take aim and fire. Especially if he crossed that line and began shooting, I knew my colleagues were in immediate life-threatening danger. The last thing I wanted to think about was being in a position where I felt like I could do something, do nothing and then someone else is hurt or worse. I was well aware of the extreme psychological state I was seconds away from being in, that I would be aiming my firearm at another human being, prepared to take his life if the situation justified it. I've heard from different sources that even the action of pointing a firearm at a person, or having one pointed at you, can have its own unexpected psychological impacts, and can affect a person long after the incident is over. But I guess until you're living in that moment, and forced to take that action, all the imagination, expectation and presumption in the world can't compare to the reality.

The stand-off continued late into the night, and the male was still showing no signs of cooperating with police. The longer it went on, the more certain I became that the only way this was going to end was with use of force. It seemed the male was finding every means to extend this incident out. Apparently, he had been charged with another offence only days earlier, and he kept wailing about his partner, or ex-partner. So clearly, this was a man at breaking point, and in his mind with nothing else to lose. It was arranged that he could speak on the phone with his father. A phone was somehow brought up to him, and he had a lengthy conversation with his father. It was communicated over the radio that STAR Force were on scene. However, they were going to remain in the background, advising where they could, but while the situation was still under control and not escalating, they would remain on scene ready to takeover if the situation intensified.

After a while, I was having doubts whether this guy had it in him to be violent towards police. He was being vocal, but the longer that went on without any show of force, the more it seemed like they were just empty threats. The requests he was making, like people he wanted to speak to were just drawing out time, as if he was digging in his heels and just being frustrating and a nuisance. To a degree, I think he was well aware of the situation he had caused, and in his own mind, feeling like all the attention was on him and he thought he was dictating all the moves and the decisions. This was his way of also holding onto that sense of control and power for as long as possible, even going so far as to say he has a firearm and will use it.

Eventually, the empty threats with no action became evident, and his perseverance was worn down. He emptied his pockets and left a few things on the roof. I was told he had some ammunition on him, and a handmade item that looked like a firearm, but was as effective as a toy. An arrest team were waiting at the foot of the ladder to take him into custody.

After the incident was over, and we were given the all clear to stand down from our positions, we were informed over radio to all meet at a designated rendezvous point, to have what's called a hot debrief, a debrief conducted in the shortest possible time after an incident is concluded. As this situation had involved numerous SAPOL sections, from STAR to Negotiators, the debrief was a valuable insight to see what feedback officers from these sections could provide in terms of how the situation was coordinated, how it was managed and any recommendations they may have for both supervisors, like sergeants and other officers. As they are experts in their own fields, and with the intricacies of complex and dangerous situations such as these, I was all ears in absorbing any new information I could gather from this rare opportunity.

As is natural after any incident, I would go through my own reflections of the situation and my performance. What were the things I did I was proud of, I could improve on for next time, and that I surprised myself in doing them. Often, my thoughts would go to the very thoughts I was having in the moment, especially when the intensity of the situation was at its peak. In this moment, the incident had the very real potential for me to draw my firearm on another human being, and if necessary, to pull the trigger. There were a couple moments in particular, where my right hand, as I talked about earlier, had felt as light as a feather in anticipation of instinctively drawing my firearm from its holster. I reflected back on my thoughts and feelings in that moment. I am a self-confessed adrenaline junkie, and anything that can fuel the fire of something exciting and make it burn brighter, then the more fun I'm having. When something intense is intensified. Now of course, I never wanted to draw my firearm, and have to use it, I would never be hoping for a situation to have to go that far. But what I reflected on, deep in my psyche in those seconds where the possibility for me to do that was very real and immediate in my mind, there had been a will to cross that line and enter into the dark unknown of my own psyche and its functioning and reaction to such an extreme action. Something I couldn't truly anticipate until you've actually lived in that place. I think the desire was not for me to have to use my firearm, but to put myself in a present state where my mind is having to comprehend the very reality of me having to cross a psychological line and do something that has the potential to fracture the very core of our psychological wellbeing and stability. Even coming so close to that action, and just being a part of the situation itself, leaves you in a surreal state. When you clock off and enter back into the normality of your world outside of work, you bring with you sometimes a newfound sense of appreciation, or coming to a new realisation, or a contrasting sense of disbelief, as you've seen the true horrors that can exist in this world, and you feel you've peaked your head behind a closed door and seen what few others have. Sometimes I would come away from shifts with a chaotic barrage of questions that I knew I didn't need the answers too, such as how people can go through their day so oblivious to the extreme dangers that exist in their same world. I could only ask myself this, because my role as a police officer meant I was always immersed in these dangers every day. Other people can choose to avoid these threats and uncomfortable occurrences as much as they want, and so to a degree, I would realise that they don't know the extent of the underbelly, because their world only exposes them to the surface. I would often have these contradicting thoughts and feelings, the deeper I got into my career, and as they would continue to resonate in my mind, at times I felt I was balancing on a tight rope, and only time would tell which way I fell, either allowing a dark cloud to cover some of my outlooks and perceptions of humanity and emotional expression, or protect my natural positivity and optimism and desire to seek and see the inspiration and light in everyone. I was finding it harder to maintain this outlook within this world.

Entering an unknown psychological space was one of my driving motivations for joining the Police. It fit in nicely with my love for the extreme and adrenaline. A sensation that your life has been fulfilled as you've been a part of things that few people can say they've ever even seen, let alone done.

Early in my career, I wasn't concerned at all about self-preservation. I wanted to be exposed to the most extreme of the extreme, unimaginable horrors that is hard for anyone to even talk about. I basically wanted to dive in headfirst, and whatever confronting reactions that may come back at me, that was a distant concern. There's something so surreal about being in an intensified situation, surrounded and faced with emotional rage, violence, emotional breakdowns. There's a mix of feeling in a hyper-present state, and an outer body sensation. That feeling I described of seeing and feeling everything happening around you but experiencing it like you're watching it through a screen like watching a movie. Dealing with death had this unnerving and eerily still feeling. Equally surreal was facing the friends or loved ones who had just found out or were only finding out from you breaking the news to them. For me, it was a disconnected experience, where I am fully aware of the emotions of others, I am fully appreciative of where they're coming from, or why they would be feeling that way, but inside me, I felt nothing, no triggers, no sentiment, and no connection to them in any emotional way. This is probably a deep dark analysis into my own psyche that even I haven't chosen to explore or understand better. Even when a hysterical mother, and the rest of the family has just arrived at a house where their son has just committed suicide. I can see clearly the emotional distress in front of me, I am deeply respectful and patient appreciating the heart-wrenching gravity of the moment, but I knew within myself, that at any moment if they were contaminating or impeding our professional duties to investigate the cause of death and circumstances around it, I could unemotionally act and do whatever I have to to preserve the scene. As was said to me by a senior, and very experienced colleague once. He told me as a police officer, you will view these situations through a very calculated, and impartial eye, a trained eye. When people are arriving at these scenes, when the incident has only just occurred, friends or family, your instinctive reaction may be to look at them with a degree of cautiousness and suspicion, because until we've conducted a thorough investigation for the coroner, and established there is no suspicious circumstances around the death, how do we know that any one of them isn't responsible, and has arrived to throw off any suspicion, or manipulate the scene? As cold, crazy, and disconnected as this may sound, this is the very real reality of policing, and the perspective a professional operator has to view these situations is one that will enable them to establish if there is someone responsible, and if in fact a crime has been committed. Observing people with empathy, but an unwaveringly clear and objective view too.

On this evening, my partner and I were called to a house where a young male had been pronounced dead by paramedics. When we arrived, there was a small group of paramedics gathered and talking. A couple of them looked tense and I gathered they were new in the role, and maybe hadn't been confronted with a dead body too much yet. We spoke to the paramedics who were first on scene and gathered any information that could assist our investigation. Part of this included some of their paperwork that provides their observations of the body, and when the person was pronounced dead. Also, other key information like had the body been moved? Who moved it? Where was he originally found and what was his physical position before being moved? All this information helps us rule out certain suspicions we may have when conducting our investigation.

We were informed the brother of the deceased, and his partner had found the male in his bedroom. No one else was home, and they were still present at the scene. They also told us they had moved the deceased from his bedroom, which was connected to a covered outdoor area, and he was on the paving just outside his bedroom door. As we entered around the rear, we were met by the male's brother and his partner. There is always that sombre mood, and I offered my condolences for their loss. Both of them were relatively calm and composed and were understanding of us having to be there and offered any cooperation they could.

My partner spoke to them, while I made my way to the deceased and the scene. Part of our investigation is thoroughly examining the deceased for any signs of fresh injuries, signs of a struggle, specific markings and tattoos, old injuries, basically determining if there is visible evidence that this person's death may be suspicious. This means getting up close and personal with the body. Being physical and hands on to move their limbs around, or role them onto their side, and to help the forensic conveyor put them in a body bag and lift them onto the bed. It's an unnerving feeling, having to move a body's limbs. Once Rigor Mortis sets in, everything becomes stiff and rigid, and that familiar sound of bones creaking as you move a stiff and waxy arm is never a sound that goes away. Any apprehension or squirminess a probationary may have in the presence of a dead body, let alone getting close and hands on with one, is quickly found out with a trip to the morgue, during our time as cadets at the Academy. This is designed for this very reason, to expose you to the reality and potentially emotionally confronting sight of seeing and touching a dead body.

Our trip to the morgue as a course had mixed emotions. A couple of cadets did find it confronting and got tearful, or kept their distance while the rest of us gathered around a few bodies, that were at different stages of decomposition. Sadly, one was a young girl, only in her early teens. I can't remember the cause of death, but I think it had only been within 24 hours. A couple of the bodies were heavily decomposed, I mean Dawn of the Dead type of stuff, ribs hanging out, skin rotten away. I hope this isn't coming across as anyway disrespectful to the deceased; it's simply describing in words what I was seeing in front of me. Most cadets could handle the sight, but that was enough for them, and they didn't need to get any closer. I remember one of my other course mates, he and I really weren't phased and taking every opportunity given by the mortuary worker to look over the bodies. Before going to the morgue, I really didn't know what my instant reaction would be. I had a strong sense of confidence that my threshold wouldn't be pushed, and that I could handle it fine. But I always keep an open mind before experiencing something I never have before. I can prepare myself as best as I can beforehand, so I feel emotionally grounded, and mentally clear and aware of any spontaneous response that may happen, but in the end, you can prepare so much, until all you can do is be completely present in the moment and allow whatever natural emotions, thoughts and feelings come too you. Then you can navigate yourself through these sensations, with a humbling sense of relief and pride, that regardless of any of it, you had the courage to show up and be there.

I can't remember how long I had been inside the deceased bedroom, beginning to take notes and drawing a mud-map of the scene, where all the furniture was, where the deceased was found and any important observations, such as prescription medication, but I heard noises coming from the front of the house, I have looked through the glass sliding door, out to the undercover back area, and saw a small number of people streaming in through the front gate. A woman was hysterical and in tears, and came running straight up to the deceased, while an elderly male close behind her, consoled her with his head down. I gathered these were the young man's parents. Funnily enough, even in this moment, I was still thinking that they may be contaminating part of our investigation, but I looked to my senior partner, and he just motioned to me to come to him. I walked out of the bedroom and tried my best to pretend I was completely invisible, as where the deceased was laying, and now with his mother crouched over him, crying out, there was very little room to pass by. As carefully and delicately as I could, I squeezed my way past and joined my partner, who quietly said something like we'll give them a few moments. The other people there were also family.

That was as sombre a mood as you could imagine, basically the young man's entire family all with him, his mother kneeling over him wailing, "No, no," his father on one knee consoling her and shaking his head, just moments after their son has taken his own life. We still had an investigation to conduct, and this was in the last half of our shift, and commonly, if you get a coroner's investigation right at the beginning of an eight-hour shift, there's a good chance that's your entire shift committed, depending on the complexities of the case. So, us only having a few hours, we still had a job to do. My partner suggested I go back inside the bedroom and continue the investigation. Just like I had exited the bedroom and squeezed past the grieving family, I tried to be invisible again and quietly shuffled my way past. I do recall, the father looking up and offering me a kind closed-mouth smile as I passed; in a moment like this, a selfless gesture like that was an honest show of his courage and character.

Gradually, my partner managed to guide everyone inside, and I was left alone in the bedroom, with the deceased laying just outside the sliding door. As I did a thorough sweep of the entire room, and attached bathroom, I was meticulous in noting any observations in chronological order as I saw them. What was noticeable was the amount of prescription medication. Some of it, bottles and boxes, were bulked up in plastic bags, and others scattered around the room, but there was a lot. Our procedure in this case is to collect all the medication, and identify the prescribing doctor, what date it was prescribed, the full quantity of the bottle or box, and the prescribed dosage to take daily. From this information, it can be easily established if the medication has played a part in the death. If a bottle of 100 capsules was purchased two days ago, with a prescribed dosage of two capsules a day, and half the bottle is empty, well…the math doesn't add up for a reason.

As I was going around the room, I couldn't help occasionally looking over to the deceased. Being there, eerily quiet, and alone with him where he died, I couldn't stop my imagination from immediately bringing to the forefront of my mind, all the walking dead movies I have seen. That may sound cold, but when you're alone with a dead body, your mind can play tricks on you. Try being in the ocean, and not letting your mind conjure up all the shark movies you've seen. So, for my peace of mind, an occasional glance back at him was reassurance enough.

At one point, I was kneeling by a coffee table, going through a plastic bag full of medication packaging. The deceased was to my right, and I could see him through my peripherals. Now, he was positioned on his back, with his hands placed resting on his chest or stomach. Out of my peripherals, I saw movement; his arm closest too me has slid from his chest and fallen by his side onto the ground. Shit! My head shot around and froze, staring at him. The silence was so eerily thick you could hear any micro whisper in the air. I slowly rose to my feet, not taking my eyes off him, and for a few seconds, I just stood there, burning my gaze into him. I had this sense that at any second, he was going to sit straight up and, in a frenzy, come charging towards me. As impossible as I'm sure it is, I've watched a lot of movies and the second I saw that arm move, all those scenarios came flooding back to me. I stood braced, ready to engage, if necessary, but of course, this was my imagination running at full sprint in the opposite direction. The arm did in-fact move, but I'm sure it was the result of his arm not resting properly on his torso, and the weight of it eventually causing it to slide off. But, when you're alone with a dead body, and you see some shit like that happen, forget what you think you know and just be ready for anything!

The rest of the night ran as smoothly as it could. We collected all the information and evidence we needed, the deceased was picked up by the forensic conveyor, and we said some departing words to the brother and his partner, before leaving the family in peace. We returned to base to complete the file. I had my lengthy and detailed 'Investigating Officer's Statement' to write up. As is one of the outstanding qualities in the police, and I'm sure emergency services alike, is the selflessness and support anyone, from any team will offer you if you reach out for it, or if they know you are swamped under. It must have been getting close to our finishing time, I think we were on arvos (afternoons) which meant we finished at 2300 hours, and nightshift started. Maybe our sergeant had mentioned something to the nightshift sergeant, but two officers, both genuine blokes and always a positive presence, who I had the upmost respect for came into the typing room and offered their assistance. With all the prescription medication we had, there was the meticulous task of counting the individual pills or capsules, recording each medication and the quantity remaining and putting the information into a table. Both officers didn't hesitate and got straight to work. I couldn't thank them enough.

We submitted our coroner's investigation and knocked off. Upon reflection, I was proud of my overall performance throughout this task. Having a grieving family right there at the scene significantly heightened the overall experience, but in those moments there's a sense of professional pride you carry, as you find in those testing times, you are able to uphold your responsibilities and execute your duties to the best of your ability and shine through as the Officer you aspire to be. I found a lot of satisfaction through some of the most intensified situations throughout my career, where in your mind, under uncertainty yet equally demanding circumstances, you have the resolve, the courage, the skills and the emotional clarity and stability to be an asset in arriving at the most desired resolution. In this particular situation, communicating with people who are suffering a heart-breaking loss, the death of their child, and remaining understanding and empathetic while sustaining your professional and emotional composure were a rewarding reflection on my performance. Also, was the depth of knowledge and experience that I now possessed. I was able to conduct most of the investigation unguided, and I had a thorough understanding of what was required for the coroner's investigation to be accepted, meaning I carried out my role with meticulous attention to detail and critical points or information. For a probationary, it's motivating to feel your confidence in any situation growing, and as your experience and knowledge of different policing procedures grows, and how you come to these decisions independently, that confidence and satisfaction grows stronger. Being exposed to the most challenging scenarios for a police officer, and once you're out of the Academy you don't have to wait long, is where so much of the challenges and valuable learning insights await. Through these real tests, you are automatically shocked into growing into the officer you envision, as instincts within yourself are forced to be expressed with full force. It's amazing when the option to hesitate is removed, and you have to rely on your training and primal instincts to execute your duties no matter what the resistance. You have to do whatever it takes to get the job done.

Chapter Thirteen

"Staring into the darkness of an emotional abyss."

The call came in right at the beginning of our shift. A young girl, in her teens, had called police, stating that her father had hit her, and he was still trying to get to her. She had had to protect herself by hiding in a pantry. We were tasked with the job, and urgently made our way to the address. Upon arrival, we entered the front door and made our way down the passage to the kitchen. We found the young girl still hiding in the pantry, and despite us saying we were police, she was hesitant to come out. As we made our way back to the front of the house, her clearly intoxicated father approached us. The girl was safe and taken outside with my partner and they stood together on the driveway, away from the front door. The father, I managed to talk him into remaining outside with me. You may be thinking, at this point, why had we not just grabbed him straight away, restrained him and taken him into custody. The thought was crossing my mind too, but my colleague had subtly told me that there was a shortage of police vehicles, and as belligerent as this guy could be, we had to buy time before we could get a cage vehicle to our location, then we would arrest him. No point wrestling with someone who is trying to resist you, without the appropriate vehicle to transport them in, and there is no way someone that intoxicated and equally irrational would be sitting in the backseat of our fleet. I quickly learned the family living there was Sudanese or a similar cultural background. The father had returned home heavily intoxicated and through an innocent remark from his daughter, that discussion had enraged him. Clearly, his deranged authority over his family was made more volatile through his intoxication, taking him to a place that resulted in assaulting his daughter. I received this information from the two sons who were also present. Both of them appeared to be in their late teens, or early twenties, and both were very appreciative for us being there, and were willing to cooperate as much as they could. As one of them told me, their father was a prolific alcoholic, and this sort of behaviour was a daily occurrence. I could see from the sunken look on his face, his posture, and the manner he spoke that he was exhausted and just over it. One of them had had to step in between his father and sister, attempting to separate them during the confrontation. The mother was also present, but I was quickly gaining clarity in my mind that the father ruled as self-proclaimed king in his house, and even as distressing as the concept of a father assaulting his daughter, the mother exerted little to no resistance or even objection.

The trouble had begun when the father, returning home in a heavily intoxicated state, and probably agitated as it was a very hot day, questioned why the portable fan had been moved. The daughter, who had seen something on YouTube and had every good intention in moving the fan to generate better air flow down the house, shared this idea with her father. The response she got was him asserting his authority and saying something like 'It's my house, you do what I say', and in his belligerent state, he tried to dominate her, grabbing her wrists and pushing her up against the wall. She stated he grabbed her and squeezed her with such force that her acrylic nails were tearing off her fingers. He struck her a few times, and she eventually got away, grabbing a kitchen knife, and barricading herself in the pantry.

I stood with the father on the front porch, while the sons were close by. I was asking the father questions, not interviewing him yet, but just giving him the opportunity to share his version of events. As reasonable as this approach may seem, given the circumstances, someone who is intoxicated, which is clearly fuel for his deeply suppressed and unresolved emotional traumas, it isn't reasonable at all. Initially, he didn't want police at his house at all, and when he came outside all he could ramble out was waving hysterically in his daughter's direction and mumbling profanities and to arrest her and get her out of here. Funny, how when I asked him what had actually happened, all he shared was his daughter coming at him with a kitchen knife. Everything that had led up to that point must have casually slipped his drunken mind, or being an emotionally scarred irrational self-proclaimed authority figure over his own family, with narcissistic tendencies and an inability to see reason beyond his own demons, perhaps he felt completely justified in him asserting his authority violently over his daughter, who had done nothing more than move a fan into an area of the house where it would provide better air flow. It's heart-breaking actually, to think that she had found this idea on YouTube, and was proud to share it with her family, knowing it would benefit them on such a hot day, only to be met with the monster within her father.

After a while, I stopped trying to get any version of events from him, his ramblings and level of intoxication weren't getting us anywhere. The best thing to do, was keep him outside, and in one place. I could see he had some unique scars across his forehead, and it occurred to me, perhaps in his home country, if it was a war-torn corner of the world, some of the horrors and traumas he may have been exposed too could contribute to his emotional damage, possibly post-traumatic stress disorder, and his heavy alcoholism was a daily coping mechanism. These were just thoughts and conclusions I was making, when observing him in his current state. Who knows, they could be the furthest thing from the truth, but his behaviour and psychology must have been affected through something over the years. His unhealthy habits, behaviour and trauma towards his family went far beyond a person with just a self-centred nature, and depicted something far more dark, sinister, and dangerous.

As the night progressed, another patrol from our team arrived, and a female colleague spoke with the daughter, while we stayed with the father. As the moment to take the father into custody drew closer, I had a quiet word with the sons. I thanked them for their cooperation and assistance, as they had been helping talk their father down when his mood would escalate. However, out of respect for them, I was realistic and open in explaining what was about to happen. I basically told them that once the cage car arrived, we would be taking their father into custody. I wanted to be as transparent with them as possible, so I told them that if their father was resistant, we would have to use necessary force to restrain him, and I acknowledged that despite them being supportive of us being there, he is still their father and seeing him in a physical confrontation like that could be distressing for them. To their absolute credit, and testament to their character and moral grounding through this entire situation, they understood this, and acknowledged that whatever we had to do, it was up to their father how it would go down.

Eventually, the cage car arrived. My partner and I acknowledged each other, and we have moved in on both sides of the father. I have informed him he is under arrest, while at the same time, positioning my hands on his right arm, ready to escort him, as my partner has done on his left side. The sons were close by, encouraging their father to just go with us. As expected, the father resisted and tried to pull his arm away from me, I have responded and tightly secured his arm behind him, pushing it high up his back. He was a relatively large man, and the three of us being on the front concrete area, didn't leave much room to move.

With him resisting, we were bearing our weight against a flimsy frame made from wood, and I could feel it giving way as we were pushing against it. My partner was securing the father's other arm, and with this in mind, I did not want to make any sudden or rapid movements that my partner wasn't prepared for. A third officer has come in to try and assist, but there wasn't enough room, and the father was only resisting and tensing up, so we began to move him off the step and across the front grass to the cage car. I think at one point, as he was looking at me, and I was in close to him, I have pushed his head away from me, thinking he might try have a crack and head butt me or spit at me.

We were trying to escort him across the grass, but he continued to resist. My partner and I still had his arms restrained behind his back, but it was clear we needed to get handcuffs on him. Both of us have taken him down onto the ground. Reactively, I have put my knee to the upper part of his back, while we have secured the handcuffs. At this point, there was probably four or five other officers standing around us, probably keeping one eye on the sons in case they took offence to their father being physically restrained. One of my colleagues, and field tutors has calmly reminded me of my knee, which I removed once the handcuffs were secured and we positioned the father into a seated position, before raising him to his feet again and escorting him to the rear of the cage car.

He remained belligerent and to me it seemed he had no real contemplation of just what this situation was. I saw a man who has been so emotionally damaged and scarred that he is acting out against the world around him by being overbearingly dominant and uncompromising, while equally irrational. While his daily intoxication would have just catapulted his armour of ego to uncontrollable extremes, which his sons had shared with me they were just over it. Seeing a grown man with absolutely no degree of resilience, or compassion for the effects of his behaviour on others, and a deep dark sense of selfishness inflamed by a traumatised mentality of victimisation is an unsettling sight, and when you combine all those ingredients together, you've got a cauldron ready to boil over.

We stood him at the back of the cage car, with the rear door open instructing him to sit on the edge and slide himself in. These instructions, or really anything we said to him were met with incoherent objections and disapproval. I used, actually in the opposite way it's meant to be, a basic self-defence move called a shoulder-turn. The actual technique enables you to turn a person in front of you enough that you can get to their side, or behind them. It requires one hand pushing on their shoulder, while your other hand pulls their other shoulder. This countering movement causes them to turn or spin off centre. When I realised that gripping his arm and trying to talk him into position wasn't working, I shoulder turned him so that he was now directly facing us, and we could force him to slide into the rear of the vehicle.

A couple of officers remained at the house to collect statements. Before driving with my colleague into the city to the City Watch House, I went back to the front porch where the two sons were still standing. I shared with them my regret that they had to see their father in that way, but I was very appreciative for their cooperation, understanding and patience. To their credit, they still found it within themselves to thank me, and my colleagues for what we had to do. The sons had been on our side from the beginning, exhausted over their father's behaviour, but I greatly respected them for the respect they were willing to show us, when they could have simply stayed completely out of it. Plus, seeing your father thrown to the ground and having strangers, police officers yes but still people you don't know, forcefully restraining him, no matter how you see him, he's still their father and not being triggered by that sight showed me that his repeated abusive behaviour had really taken its toll on his family.

We arrived at the City Watch House, unloaded our equipment as protocol requires, and prepared to escort the father into a holding cell, while we then informed the Charging Sergeant we had arrived. It was clearly evident that the father's demeanour was not going to improve. I attempted to search him while we were in the holding cell, but just like back at the house, he became resistant and argumentative, refusing to follow any direction and rambling or just yelling loud noises. He sat himself on the floor of the cell and was flaying his arms everywhere. Instead of trying to grab one of his arms, I've basically put his arm in a headlock, scooping my right arm under his armpit and pulling my arm threw so I could lock it in and grab my belt buckle. Another officer caught onto what I was doing and did the same thing, and together we've dragged the father out of the cell, down the hall and into the padded holding cell, which is basically a large square room with padding floor to ceiling, reserved for those less cooperative, at risk or more enthusiastic detainees.

Anytime a detainee is in the holding cell, they always require a set of eyes on them at all times, which means one of you commences the charging procedure and paperwork, and the other watches the detainee. This is crucial, because so often we'd hear stories of detainees pulling something concealed and potentially dangerous that was missed during searches. The worst story I heard, from one of my original field tutors, was something that he witnessed first-hand. He told me a story of a detainee who appeared anxious and tense and was pacing in the cell. Suddenly, the detainee has stood on the raised cement block, that has a thin mattress, you might call it a bed, and has calmly swan dived headfirst onto the concrete floor, cracking their skull wide open. This story always stayed with me, so when it was my turn to monitor any detainee, that's where my attention was. I didn't want to be responsible for missing a concealed item, or someone injuring themselves or worse, because I was distracted or not as attentive as I could be.

Now, it was the father and me in the padded room. The door to the hallway is always opened, but it's basically watching over a person whose abusive, aggressive, out of control and will say anything that comes to mind to try set you off or get what they want. He was a drunken mess, wailing and rolling all over the ground. At one point, as he was incoherently wailing, he's rolled towards me, where I was standing in the doorway. I've put my foot out, and placed it on his back, preventing him from rolling any further. I wasn't aggressive, or even assertive, and I think for a moment, I just felt a sense of emptiness and numb, watching this fully grown man, knowing what he's put his family through, and seeing in front of me the depth of his emotional trauma and complete absence of any resilience or self-worth. When I put my foot out, and the situation in front of me as it was, I think the feeling that was going through me was actually one of disgust and thinking it was pathetic. Despite deep traumas that he was probably harbouring from earlier chapters in his life, this man was putting his family through a nightmare every day. On this night, for no reason whatsoever other than his own intoxicated inflated ego, he had attacked and assaulted his own daughter. I think because it had been such a long night already, and we had been babysitting this man, and managing his behaviour for the entire time, my tolerance and empathy towards him was depleted to non-existent levels. This situation didn't last long, as one of the sergeants from the charging bay had seen what was happening on CCTV and came running in, dragging the father back into the middle of the room and giving him a verbal berating. I think it was at this point, that the father tried to resist, and his behaviour escalated. I felt bad that the sergeant felt like they had to come in and manage this guy when I was there the entire time. I gathered the sergeant wanted to get this guy back into handcuffs, so I jumped into position and secured his left arm and locked it behind his back. Another officer did the same to his other arm, and we secured him and sat him up.

My memory of the rest of the night is slightly faded. Funnily enough, I do recall when we got him in front of the Charging Sergeant, he had sobered up and was surprisingly polite and compliant. I was looking at him, in a slightly bewildered way, as he was responding to the sergeant's questions, thinking what you've just done tonight, and what you've put us through for the last few hours. This side of him was practically civilised, even soft spoken and respectful. This was a case of Jekyll and Hyde as a result of alcohol. I had seen it a few times on Hindley Street. The person will be arrogant, defiant, and full of bravado. Then, once they've been at the Watch House and had a chance to sober up, they are humbled, sheepish, courteous and sometimes even apologetic and ashamed. Sadly, that can be a dark and damaging side of an addiction, or just over-consumption of a substance, until the person is left with the shame and guilt of the trauma and nightmare that others have been dragged through as a result of their inner-darkness being unleashed.

A few months later, when I was back at the father's house, following up statements from the family members who were present that night, I was talking to one of the sons and the mother came to the door. They were reluctant to cooperate, and probably just wanted the event to be behind them and have no further input, especially when you're living in the same house as the offender. As I was finishing up the conversation, the father emerged and stood behind the others. He was civilised and even said hi as I walked away. Coming across offenders you have had previous dealings with was always surreal, just be polite professional and on your way, but no matter how respectful they may be, and in this case, he was clearly in a sober state, I would always remain vigilante knowing I had seen their inner beast before, their dark demons and what they can become when they've lost control and are slipping over the edge, knowing that beneath the surface, they had the potential to be a danger, to themselves and others.

Life as a police officer very quickly raised my sense of situational awareness and vigilance when I wasn't in uniform. I had in my mind places I had no desire to pass through if I could avoid them, and if I was there, I was face-checking everyone and got in the habit of always scanning, to avoid the possibility of seeing a character I knew, or who may know me. Having said that though, I never felt if I saw someone I had dealt with, that there would be any animosity or aggression. I had always ensured I was as accommodating and respectful as possible. Of course, when the duty required certain action, I was all in, but even then, the seasoned criminals were as understanding of our obligations as we were. I remember being told of a story at the Academy, by a senior detective who was speaking with our course. We were discussing professional courtesy and the importance of maintaining that respect, empathy, and humanity for anyone we dealt with. He shared a story of a colleague decades ago when he had still been serving in the United Kingdom (UK). His colleague had had to arrest a gang-member, a part of a notorious street gang at the time. Regardless of what the incident was over between the officer and the offender, the officer was professional, courteous, respectful, and patient with him. Sometime after, this officer, off-duty, entered a pub for a drink. A group of gang-members were in the pub and recognised this officer and started to hassle him. However, with the group was the male that the officer had dealt with on that prior occasion. The male has stepped in, told his crew to back off, this guy was okay, and they let him be. Because of this officer's civilised and respectful behaviour towards this male, that established a degree of respect, which in this particular case saved the officer some trouble. Had his attitude and treatment of the male been vastly different, this situation could have been a lot more severe for him. This reminds me of a saying I've heard, "You can tell a lot about a person, by how they treat those they don't have to treat nicely." Meaning, despite someone else's attitude and behaviour, it reflects a great deal of strength, self-awareness, emotional intelligence, and mental fortitude for a person to remain composed and empathetic in the face of someone trying to verbally, and physically tear them down. The interactions we have with others, is our legacy in the making, and the effect we have on others is how we'll be remembered. I always took it as a comfort that if I am as professionally respectful towards everyone I encounter, then I can breathe a sigh of relief and not feel such a necessity to be looking over my shoulder, even when I am off-duty. Now, I always remained aware that regardless of my good intentions and choosing to believe in the goodness and goodwill of others, to some it doesn't really matter how you treat them, if your back is turned, or if you foolishly drop your guard, they may very well try to run you over. I remained vigilante enough, that I would always give someone the benefit of the opportunity to do right if I ever crossed paths with them out of uniform (this never actually happened during my career), but I knew if this allowance was abused or discarded, then they have woken the bear.

Humanity is something to be celebrated. We as a species are synonymous with inspiring within ourselves, the greatest depths of our capabilities. We are responsible for recognising something as impossible, and we're always the ones who prove ourselves wrong by raising the bar beyond what we ever preconceived as possible. We're our own greatest accomplishment, with the limitless potential to construct and achieve whatever our minds are capable of believing, if only through action and consistency. We also have the potential, to bring horrors and depravity into this world unspeakable in nature. The mind can be as limitless as the sky, and drive us to shine brighter than the sun, or it can be a bottomless abyss of darkness that can disgust us at the very sight of our own reflection or convince us that we're not even worthy of another breath. It has the power to bring anything we can dream of to life, almost like a magic wand if you're willing to wave it with patience, consistency and hard work, or it can manifest from within nightmares, ghouls and horrors that clutch and claw at our psyche and distort our very own sense of self-identity. I found during my time in uniform, that I saw both extremes of the human spectrum. People accomplishing and capable of heroic degrees of courage, that they displayed daily as matter-of-factly that it was so unconscious and natural to them, and of course those who had been falling into the depths of that emotional abyss since being introduced to this world, and either had no control over even themselves, or only saw the world, society, and every person as a source of hatred and responsible for who they were and what had happened to them in their life. In their own mind, a victim for life.

Right up until the very end of my policing career, I was still capable of seeing both sides in a person. One side, I could see very clearly on the surface, in who they were and how they presented to the world and the other, I chose to see and believe could exist somewhere within them. What I started to notice, and it was dependent on perhaps the job we were dealing with, and definitely the person, or people we were encountering. What I became aware of was my empathy in these moments was non-existent. I had no regard for what may happen to this person if we had to escalate our force to control the situation. I felt a degree of numbness in the moment, disconnect to them and the situation around me, but equally ready to execute the full extent of my force, and whatever the outcome to another person as a consequence, I believed I wouldn't have any regret, empathy or any emotion about it whatsoever. The only time I had to utilise one of my tactical options at a tasking (besides training) was against an injured animal. Yet what I still found curious after this incident, was the absence of any afterthought or even temporary psychological reactions, let alone repercussions. As dark and as scary as it may sound to say it out loud, but that's one of the reasons I began writing this was to explore with raw honesty and accountability, the true depths of this psychological journey for me in this extreme and confronting world. When I executed that animal, it could have been a person to me, if of course my actions were necessary and justified, such as to preserve the life of innocence, my colleagues or myself.

Chapter Fourteen

"I've found it…it went through a back fence. Bullet Holes and brotherly love."

We were at the beginning of a nightshift when a tasking came through that someone had reported hitting a kangaroo with their car. If we took this tasking, I instantly knew that the responsibility of pulling the trigger and executing the animal would fall on me. I was partnered with my field tutor, whom I had worked with consistently for most of my time at Holden Hill, and a new probationary to our team. She was early in her probation so it wouldn't be fair entrusting her with something this confronting so early, especially since I had never done it before. I knew whether I liked it or not, there was no getting out of it. Sure enough, we responded to the call.

We arrived in a quiet suburban street where a car was parked, and a small group of people gathered. They all confirmed they were in the vehicle, and I firstly ensured that everyone was okay. I then asked what had happened, and one of them explained a kangaroo had collided with them around the side of their bonnet as they were travelling at about 50 kilometres. I was already expecting to see the animal in the nearby grass, unable to move if it had survived at all, but there was no sign of it. I began to think maybe I've dodged a bullet on this one (poor timing for a pun like that) as it looks like its continued off somewhere. If we can't find it, I can't kill it. The group stayed by the car, and my field tutor and I spread out to cover more ground. There was a two-storey house, with an open front garden, but still no sign of the roo (kangaroo). Next to this house was a vacant block, that extended down past the house and around the back of it, opening up into an open grassed area. It was mainly made up of dirt and shrubbery, and as it was in the middle of the night, we were relying on our torch lights. As I was searching this area, I was met with an unexpected sight. The roo was definitely still alive, and on the move. It had hopped into this open block and further down towards the back opening. However, it was moving very gingerly, and didn't have that spring in its step you might think when it's sensing movement and trying to get away.

As it wasn't moving too fast, even with our presence close by, we visually assessed it as best we could. We could see what appeared to be blood around both its ankles. I kept it within sight, while my field tutor made some calls. A short time later, a man from Flora and Fauna Rescue arrived. He made his own inspection of the roo, confirming that both its ankles were broken. In so many words, he confirmed, yet, it will have to be terminated. So, that bullet I thought I had dodged earlier, now was going to be fired from my own sidearm, with me pulling the trigger and executing a living creature. Now for some, this may not be much of an issue. I know people go out shooting and spotlighting as fun in their free time and people from the country or have lived on farms. For some, it's a daily chore, no more outstanding than doing the laundry. But when this is a new occurrence, and you're drawing a lethal weapon from its holster and using it, in an uncontrolled environment, there is some tensions that arise and as you're about to learn, those tensions can be exasperated when the simple objective of pulling the trigger once becomes increasingly more complicated.

Now that we knew we were going ahead with terminating the animal, we had to ensure we were minimising risk as much as possible and all the safety considerations were in place. Ear plugs were a necessity. By now, the roo had moved further down the open area and was near more of an open park grassed space. Determining the potential trajectory and path of the round was important, and so positioning myself so that there was as much clear space behind the roo and around us as possible. The closest houses and backyards were about 100 metres behind us. That was another thing, the roo was still standing. I hadn't even visualised this when the prospect of having to execute the animal entered my mind. I instantly thought it would be laying on the ground, unable to move much and I simply fire a round down at it. At this point, the roo was about five to seven metres from me, standing and looking at me.

The man from Flora and Fauna gave me a quick briefing, saying the best thing to do was imagine drawing a line between its eyes, and a vertical line straight down the middle of this. In the centre of that vertical line, just above the eye level is the best target. In case you don't know, kangaroos have very small brains, and I had heard police stories, one in particular, where it took about five rounds to the head to terminate a roo. The other rounds just bounced around in its skull, causing it pain and panic. I was determined then, to end its suffering with a single round, and with as little fuss as possible.

Everyone, the guy from Flora and Fauna Rescue, my field tutor, and our other Probie all stood behind me. With the ear plugs in, all I could hear was my breathing. I drew my firearm and tried to relax my grip, but amazing how the training we receive kicks in so automatically. As I drew, I kept it close to my torso, pull it to my sternum and then push it out in front of me to be as central as possible with my line of sight. I tried to slow my breathing, the roo was staring straight at me, so I took aim between its eyes, eased pressure on the trigger and fired a single round, nothing.

The roo was still staring at me, still standing as if nothing had happened. I lowered my weapon, as if its pointing at someone's belt buckle instead of their head and assessed. I remained completely calm and composed. The job wasn't done, and this was my responsibility, so I had to calm my flurry of thoughts and internal 'oh shits' that were going on and reassess. I took aim again, same target and fired another round. This time the roo's head jolted a tiny bit, but not the intended effect I was wanting. I could hear the guy from Rescue calmly talking and suggesting I reposition myself. I took a few steps and came around on the side of the roo. A third round that hit its jaw, but it was still standing. A fourth that hit around its chest, and after staggering a bit it fell to the ground. Finally, a fifth round to its head to finish it off, yeah, with as little fuss as possible!

The Rescue guy came over and assessed the roo. I was relieved to find out that all five of my rounds had been on target. Unexpectedly though, the first two had gone exactly where I intended them too, but both had skimmed completely off the skull. If you're thinking this is a cop-out for me to cover the fact that I completely missed the roo from about five metres away, well, there were two distinct grazes where the hair from the roo's forehead was gone, in the moment the rounds had shaved its head. But this meant, we had to locate the rounds and confirm where they had landed.

My field tutor ventured off into the quiet night towards the backyard fences that were about 80–100 metres away. Then, those words that sent a cold shiver straight through me. He had found it, or at least the first bullet hole where it had entered through a rear fence. The second was in the other fence at a 90-degree angle to the first one. Then, it appeared the round had lost speed, hit the outside of a shed, and come to rest between the fence and the shed, which, as we would discover was actually a rec-room/leisure area for the occupants of that home. The relief washed over me that things had not turned out a million times worse, but then there was the need to talk to the home occupants and explain everything.

The occupant of the first property was a lovely elderly woman who was deaf, who obviously hadn't heard a thing and was very obliging. She took us to the backyard, and we located the entry point and assessed for any other signs of damage. The other occupants were a family with some friends around. My field tutor did all the talking and went out the back with the occupants to retrieve the round. I'm sure they thought it was hilarious and probably gave them talking material for the remainder of their evening.

As we were driving back to base, despite some banter from my field tutor and our other Probie with us, I felt quietly confident and reassured upon reflection of the situation. I was playing it over a thousand times in my head, scrutinising every possible second of how things had played out. But the more I relived everything, the more at ease I felt if I had to answer to anyone or if I was walking into a roasting. The Flora and Fauna Rescue guy had instilled in me enough positive feedback and compliments to reprioritise my own self-judgements. Speaking with him beforehand, he had explained he is a firearms instructor, so besides myself and my colleagues, I was under the watchful eye of a subject matter expert. As I'm writing this, reflecting on the moments and more specific details come back to me, I actually recall him saying to me as we were all about to leave, that if I was scrutinised or called up in front of anyone to answer for any of this, that he would be willing to go in and bat for me and verify as a witness, that all safety measures had been assessed and put into place and that the two rounds off the skull were a result of, as he explained it, the wrong tool for the job. When we assessed the roo afterwards, he explained that the most efficient firearm for this job would have been a shotgun. He stated the rounds in our firearms had a reputation of this happening, but I didn't want to make excuses for myself. However, with his knowledge of wildlife, humane disposal of them and firearms, it gave me a quiet sense of reassurance. Plus, the relief that from a short distance, all my rounds had been on my target.

He also went through his own observations of the situation as a whole, and really had only positives to say. We had diligently assessed our surrounds to ensure as much risk to surrounding properties could be minimised as much as possible. We ensured it was as controlled environment as it could be when handling a firearm in a suburban setting. Despite my first and second shots not getting the result I had intended on, I remained cool and composed, I reassessed and repositioned myself, while all the while remaining patient with myself and not allowing emotions or hesitations to wash over me, and all my rounds were on target.

Back at base, both my field tutor and I completed reports of the incident. From memory, he covered some of the more in-depth material, such as the damage caused to private property, as SAPOL would need to be covering damages. With his assistance, I completed a statement of the event, one that ensured every detail of our preparation, performance and risk assessments was meticulously explicit, so that anyone reading the statement who wasn't present at the time would have no doubt in their minds that every precaution to mitigate the risks had been taken into account. We even included photographs of the roo, to confirm that all five rounds were on target. In the end, the report was accepted with no repercussions (the assessing officer even emailed us back saying the photos weren't necessary for next time).

As a police officer, there's no boundaries to what you may be exposed too, and no matter how surreal, confronting, terrifying, violent, extreme or traumatic, you're the solution to a problem that has transcended into all out chaos. In the most extreme circumstances, this could mean people get hurt or worse.

On this night, we were called to a domestic disturbance, with reports of a knife involved. Anytime this information came back, before arriving on scene, we would pull over and vest up. These are the bulletproof vests that we carry in our fleets. The vests we wore as part of our uniform, that carried most of our tactical equipment, was meant to be slash proof, but would do nothing against a stab, let alone a gunshot. We arrived on scene with other officers. Standing in the front yard was a male standing up with a female hugging him. I think he was shirtless, and as we got into better lighting, I could see blood splattered all over him. He appeared unassumingly calm, even disconnected. The information we had received was it was the brother who had attacked the male. Then, another male walked out of the front door. At first instance, he appeared blank in his face, like he was looking through everything and not particularly focused or really aware. I said something like is that your brother? Knowing full well the suspect was still on the scene, and for all we know could still have a knife or anything and still be in a rage. I directed the male to stand over by the front outside wall of the house, which he did and sat against a ledge. He did not appear emotional, defiant, arrogant. He did not appear to be anything, just an empty shell of a person, not expressing any emotions. Other officers had arrived with us, and it was very clear this was as serious an offence as you could get before actually murdering someone. Officers went into the house to grab details of others inside, while others attended to the victim, who was suffering multiple stab wounds. Although you wouldn't have known it from his demeanour, but shock can have a powerful ability to disconnect someone emotionally and physically from the shear severity and gravity of the trauma they've just suffered. Another officer was shadowing me with the suspect, and we wrapped his hand and his shoe with paper bags to preserve the evidence, that being the blood from the victim, that was splattered over him. We searched him and took him to the back of the cage vehicle. With a major indictable offence like this, it's important to get a video camera on the suspect as quickly as possible, and verbally caution them even faster so that anything they may say can be used as admissible evidence in court. Amazing how a simple verbal paragraph can carry so much legal weight and responsibility:

"The recording device has now been activated; the time is on 'date' my name is Probationary Constable Betts, ID 77356. In company with me is (any other officers present), I now ask all other persons' present to state their name and date of birth (any other civilians) can you please state your full name and date of birth (to the suspect)? I am now going to ask you some further questions which are being video recorded, you are not obliged to answer them, but anything you say may be given in evidence. Do you understand?"

Without verbally stating, or writing any of this legally binding declaration, you could interview a suspect for four hours, and not a single word or confession can be used in court. Without this caution, anything they say is completely inadmissible, as useless as if they didn't even make a sound.

As I was standing, facing the suspect who was sitting in the back of the cage vehicle, as soon as I got the camera on him, I cautioned him with the relevant information, however, he may as well have been 1000 miles away, as if he didn't even hear me, the words were just white noise, and he probably wasn't even aware of my presence. Looking at him and speaking with him, he was psychologically disconnected from the reality happening around him. I remember he started yelling his brother's name, looking over my shoulder as if trying to get his brother's attention, and he asked me about three or four times which station we were going too? I informed him the first couple times, we would be transporting him to the Adelaide City Watch House. But he kept asking me, literally every couple of minutes, as if he had the memory of a goldfish and couldn't even recall already asking me that same question, or the words I was giving him were just not being heard. With the violence of the crime, it appeared he was psychologically distant. As it was just me and him, while everyone else was running around gathering evidence and witness statements, I found it fascinating to observe this male. He appeared small and timid, perhaps not a very well-developed intellect, let alone an emotional understanding of himself, and how to regulate or self-moderate his own emotional reactions, and the subsequent actions fuelled by these outbursts. I learnt in this role, seeing it first hand and dealing with suspects, when you combine perhaps an upbringing of chaos, where they're seeing family figures in their life acting with violence to solve a problem, such as bashing their partner, rather than the emotional intelligence, and self-awareness to modulate your own frustrations and discuss in a mild-mannered way to seek a solution. Or the use of alcohol and substances to mask and escape from that very chaos, breeding more frenzied acting out and dysfunction, I learnt that violence to some of these people, no matter how steep the scale of it, was as reactive an action as slamming your fist on a table during an argument. The very idea of picking up a knife, or any object and using it to inflict severe damage and injury on another person goes against the very fibre of our own beings. When you subtract those learned boundaries and restrictions out of the equation, all you're left with is that chaos where the extent of damage, triggered by as little as a passing thought through one's mind, is never even considered, let alone the consequences they may face if they inflict that damage.

I was looking at a guy right now who none of that would have even echoed in his mind. I found it hard to even picture this timid, scrawny scruff even appearing intimidating holding the knife, or how he would even appear in that moment of savagery and violence. For most of the time that he was sitting there, and I was watching him, we didn't say much. Once we'd dropped him at the Watch House, a couple of CIB Detectives took over from us, and we were back on the road.

Chapter Fifteen

"Well, this is messed up."

Some jobs are a lot more testing than others, or the nature of them just makes them a lot more messed up and hard to comprehend than others. Often, anything involving children was high in this regard, especially if they've been exposed to extreme violence or emotional intensity. I had heard of stories of officers who could no longer attend jobs involving children if they're a parent themselves. The shear graphic nature of seeing a child in such poverty, or in a harsh circumstance would hit a little too close to home for them and for their own psychological wellbeing, they just couldn't expose themselves to that. I never worked with any officer like this, and not having any children myself, I could only deeply respect if they've come to that realisation and have to make that choice to continue to function in the role. Then again, working alongside an experienced officer with about 12 years' experience who was a father himself, seeing him in action where children were heavily involved, clearly he was able to disassociate his own love and connection to his own children when present in the trauma and chaos of this job.

I was partnered up with a solo patrol in my team, to provide assistance for a tasking that had just come in. The Department of Child Protection (DCP) were attending the address of one of their cases, to remove the children from the parents. As I learned, these decisions are not made lightly, and they're often the end result of a lot of investigating, and a lot of justification why such a decision is necessary. In this case, both parents had lengthy criminal records, they were still heavily active in criminal behaviour as well as substance abuse. To support the DCP were a couple SAPOL members from Family Violence (FV) who also have a very active part in these investigations. However, the decision to remove the children, that burden fell on the DCP. My colleague and I were there to add support to the operation and intervene and provide backup to FV and the DCP if the situation escalated. We arrived at a rendezvous point, where DCP and FV met us to go over the objectives of the operation, and what actions may be necessary. Once we all got back in our vehicles and made our way to the nearby address, we were just around the corner when a Commodore sedan came speeding around the corner and then made a quick turnaround another corner just in front of us. We caught up with the vehicle not far up that street. It was believed that the couple knew they were being paid a visit and had gotten their children into the car and tried to make a run for it. FV members had seen both parents in the car, yet when we all caught up with them, besides the kids, only the mother was in the car. The suspicion was, as the father must have had a warrant out for his arrest, they had pulled over just before we all caught up with them, and he'd made a run for it, while she denied he was ever there. Anyway, this was quickly overlooked, as the purpose for all of us being there was simply for the children.

The DCP members, who obviously knew the mother, began talking to her and explaining the situation. The mother made it very clear, that that was not an option, and as the reality of the situation began to sink in with her, she gradually became more defiant and forward that it was not an option that her children were being taken. By now, she was out of the car and pacing irritably, agitated at the presence of all of us there. She made a phone call, completely ignoring and talking over the DCP members. Apparently, it was her mother on the phone, their grandmother, and she was explaining the situation too her. In a short time, the grandmother had arrived and began to have discussions, with her daughter, DCP and FV. I spoke to another woman, it could have been the sister of the mother, who did not take offence to us being there, and she was on reasonable terms with talking to the mother. While everyone was talking, I spoke to her realising she may be a peaceful mediator who could have some influence on the mother, and reason with her, convincing her to make a decision that would not see the situation become volatile.

Eventually, a compromise was arrived at between the grandmother, the mother, DCP and FV that everyone would return to the house, just around the corner so more discussions could continue. As the grandmother had a fair bit of influence of this decision, I get the feeling she was realising there was only one outcome, and it would be best to have her daughter in the comfort and safety of their home, so she could be consoled and kept under some of the family's watchful eye.

We all returned to the house. The DCP members, the mother, grandmother, and the children all went inside the house to continue talking. I think the female

FV member accompanied them. Some time had passed, and the mother came back out into the small paved front outdoor area the rest of us were waiting. Her demeanour did not appear to have improved; in fact, she seemed more worked up and becoming more emotional by the minute. She was making it very clear, that she would fight if anyone tried to take her children. At one point, my partner, putting on his firm assertive police voice, made the mother's options very clear. He had done checks and saw that she had a warrant out for her arrest. He informed her that if her behaviour did not subside, and if she continued to resist and be defiant, then we had the authority to arrest her and take her away anyway. He did not want to execute that warrant and was willing to overlook it if she cooperated with the DCP and FV.

Things went on like this for a little longer. Ultimately, the more time that passed without her cooperating, the more likely things were going to escalate, and only get worse. One way or another, as much as she was hysterical and protesting, the children or herself were going to be removed. Things were quickly spiralling out of control, and I had moved myself into a position where I was by the mother's side. The male member of FV, who was on her other side, looked at me in a way that confirmed enough was enough. He has grabbed her arm, triggering me to grab her other arm. She tensed up but was not going to cooperate. We ended up walking her over to a nearby wall of the house to stabilise her, so we could get her arms handcuffed behind her back. For whatever reason, this was not working. She was hysterical, and we didn't have enough control over her. Next thing I remember is her and I moving away from the wall. I have brought her down to the ground. She has started screaming she has had a caesarean in the past few weeks. With her hands now cuffed, I have quickly gotten her onto her side, and eventually into a seated position. More discussion followed, and it was clear to the mother that this situation was not going to end the way she wanted. She has requested to say goodbye to her children before we took her. This was the most fucked up moment of this entire tense situation. The details of this moment, and the thoughts I had in that exact moment are as clear to me as if they happened an hour ago. She is seated, cross-legged with her hands handcuffed behind her back, wailing and crying hysterically, while her mother, holding perhaps the youngest of her children (he couldn't have been older than three) leans down, and with a blank look on his face that indicates he's well aware of the chaos, processing it, but still too young to understand what it all means, gives his mother a kiss on the forehead while she is crying out. I was

146

standing on her right side, hands on her back and shoulders to ensure she did not spring to her feet (which at one point she had done so quickly, it came as a surprise, like an explosion of raw emotions and adrenaline have lifted her too her feet). At that moment, while restraining this hysterical woman, and watching the face of her toddler son kiss her to say goodbye, I remember thinking to myself, *Yeah, well this is completely fucked up.* The very situation, all the elements that had collided together to create the furnace we were all engulfed in seemed as unnatural a thing to occur as I could ever imagine. It was like a tear had been made in the very fabric of the universal blanket, that protects us all from seeing and hearing things that our minds and senses are never meant to experience, and for those few moments the concept of natural order and balance were thrown away and something seriously devastating to human beings crept into our reality. I describe this in this kind of emotive detail, only because of the presence of such a young child. For that child to give his mother the natural loving affectionate gesture of a kiss on the forehead, while she is emotionally breaking down, and being restrained by police, in my mind there was no situation that was more unnatural and disturbing.

My partner and I took the woman down to our vehicle. She was still in hysterics, and being a larger woman, and who was not currently in a state to support herself, it took all my might to keep her from collapsing on the ground and get her into the backseat. My partner and I both tried to console her with positive reinforcement that she would be seeing her children again soon. My colleague, who has children of his own used this connection as a means to build a bridge with her and establish some empathy and rapport. By the time we were back at the Holden Hill Watch House, her demeanour had calmed down a lot and she was cooperative, and I think even somewhat relieved as the reassurance we had been offering, must have allowed the raw shock and intensity of not seeing her children again subside to the reality that that wasn't the case.

Chapter Sixteen

"For Plap's sake."

The kangaroo incident was only a few months out from my official resignation from the South Australia Police. For some time now, actually looking back, right at the beginning of my probation, and even a few fleeting contemplations I had while at the Academy, I had been wrestling more and more with my own unrest and a growing realisation that I didn't mesh within the world of policing. This is in no way a discredit to any of the individuals I worked with or colleagues I was working alongside. The police are a mixing pot of so many personality types, from an array of all walks of life and generations. I can only remember receiving support, encouragement, patient guidance and warmth from anyone I either worked with on the same team every day, or even asking a simple question to someone passing by. In fact, before I delve deeper into this topic, writing this brings back so many of those interactions with other officers who would in an instance, direct their time, attention, and energy towards me and whatever the task it was I was seeking help for. If I was in the typing room, they would stop what they were doing, sit down and assist for as long as it took before I got it. Plus, if there was an element of time pressure involved, such as a submission, so many would prioritise your work over themselves, and take on any of the workload to help submit the work faster. I remember, one time on Hindley Street, I was working in the typing room on an investigation for an offence I didn't have much experience in. An obliging officer assisted me for at least two hours. I say assist, but he practically did everything and not once did he appear impatient or frustrated at the prospect of missing out on valuable hours of his own working time to assist a Probie.

Leaving a legacy, you believe is an accurate reflection of you, and by that, I mean where you feel people were able to recognise and witness the very best qualities and potential within you. This can be a greater sense of fulfilment, even more so than a perceived outcome or result. Possessing self-awareness or developing it through intention and deliberate effort enables you to reflect on the quality of a legacy you've left, and the intention, the attitude and the presence you choose to show up into that environment every single day. As joining the police had meant so much to me, and for so long, when my opportunity finally came, I was very intentional about how I showed up, how I felt I would be seen as a person, how I faced conflict and challenges and what qualities I wanted my seniors and colleagues to associate with me. In this regard, I am very proud of the legacy I left in each chapter throughout my SAPOL story. I think that's where a legacy, and self-awareness are very closely aligned. A legacy can be a masterpiece left behind, after a person left their final brush stroke on the canvas. A masterpiece can only be completed with an intentional purpose, a vision in one's own mind, while they stare into a blank canvas. They have a vision of what they want to transform that canvas into, and then with time, commitment, and an accountability to one's own commitment to the intentions they bring to each stroke, and meticulous effort, eventually, your masterpiece, your legacy can be fulfilled.

I knew throughout my SAPOL journey that the impressions I was making were aligned with the vision of myself and the light I wanted to be seen in. That simply, I was fulfilled with the version of myself that I brought into every situation and interaction. Of course, we can't dictate the perception of ourselves in the eyes of others. We can't tell them how to see us as a person. However, we can believe within ourselves who that person is everyday that's showing up and facing the world. Knowing that person is presenting with the best intentions, and that we haven't compromised ourselves or given an effort that we know is beneath our greatest capabilities. A person who is genuinely kind, connective and emotionally intelligent (EQ) in nature can be perceived by another as weak or gentle, if this other person's very nature is built on qualities and behaviours that are vastly different. A male with great depth and development in both self-awareness and EQ may not be well received by another who's hard-headed and whose very core was grounded early in life that to try to understand one's own emotions, let alone converse and express them is seen as showing weakness. At times, I encountered this, sometimes to extremes in others and their disdain for someone verbalising complex emotional insights was simply born from a complete lack of understanding all together. Or even, through repeated abuse and traumas, exploring those very concepts was fear-inducing, and forcing them to stare into the dark abyss of their own psyche, an idea and a place that terrified them.

When I was still on Hindley Street, I was a few months into my probation, and there were a couple of my performance standards that were not developing at the rate SAPOL, or my field tutors wanted. This simply meant that certain dates were extended out, and more effort and attention, by my field tutors was focused into supporting me to develop in these lacking areas. I admit, from early on I was sensing there were expectations and requirements within the role that were feeling unnatural and forced to me, but being new into this profession, and with so many skills and procedures to absorb, I reassured myself that this was perfectly natural when you're new into such a demanding and complex role.

One day, while driving around with my field tutor, we discussed some of this, and some of what he said gave me comfort, that despite being 'delayed' in some of my development, it was my personal presence, my likeable self, my consistent humbled willingness to be coached, guided, take criticism and the respect I had amongst my colleagues, plus all the while always showing up with a positive and optimistic manner, that he said made my field tutors, my seniors want to go above and beyond in seeing me successful and crossing the finish line. Like he said, if my attitude was different, such as not having a positive optimistic approach to my learning, and my struggles, he said people wouldn't be willing to invest their time and energy in supporting me. Or even worse, possessing a sense of arrogance and know-it-all beyond the scope of my current capabilities. So many times, he'd seen Probies who carried an element of swagger or even arrogance during their time coming up. They weren't coachable and felt like they had all the answers. Someone like this doesn't warrant others to exert themselves further or overly invest more in their success.

When the decision was made to relocate me from Hindley Street to Holden Hill, it came as a surprise to my sergeants, and of course to me. Like I discussed earlier, they had been informed of this decision moments before I walked into the office to hear the news. In that moment, with your superiors' eyes on you, being told that your performance is dictating a decision like this with the intention of further supporting your improvement, it's so easy to feel like a special case, or in your own mind, I hate to say it, but a failure. Especially with my sergeant and brevet sergeant sitting in the room watching as this news is landed on you for the first time. However, this is one of those moments where my legacy within the workplace was carved in stone. I remember feeling some of those cold clammy sweats starting to brew within me when you're sitting in front of a panel, and either being criticised or being told something that is easy for you to feel uncomfortable about hearing. In this exact moment, feeling the eyes of everyone around you, almost feeling the heat exuding from their gaze, and becoming hyper self-conscious knowing full well that they're looking for a reaction from you, elicited by the gravity of the news you're receiving. It was in this exact moment that I knew the promise I had made to myself, the contract I had signed in my mind to uphold, to be consistent in my presence and demeanour, to be known for my attitude and my qualities, yes by those I work with, but most importantly to inspire that sense of fulfilment within me, this was a crucial time to uphold that contract.

As I heard the news, I didn't reflect any animosity, in my face or my body language, I didn't fidget, scoff or indicate any sign of insult. I responded with a sense of acceptance, respect and understanding that was also true to myself. Not just holding back any anger or frustration, but genuinely projecting my acceptance of the decision, the extent of my resilience, and my willingness to embrace this new obstacle as just another opportunity for my self-improvement, right or wrong the decision.

Naturally, after the initial moment, there's always waves of realisations and comprehension as the full weight of the decision starts to sink in. Through this time, internally some of your justified frustrations start to speak their mind, in your mind. They snatch the microphone away from your consciousness and, step into the spotlight at the forefront of your mind and make themselves heard. This is our ego talking, a basic human nature anytime we receive news we weren't expecting, or that we don't entirely agree with. As I'm always learning in life, the key is how long you allow that influence to stand in the spotlight and speak. Do you sit in the audience in stunned silence, giving it all the power and the time to say exactly what it feels, and just being persuaded by its one-dimensional opinion? Or do you accept its frustration, impartiality, and patiently to enable you to then contradict its response with a more constructive perspective that is remaining true and grounded to yourself and your willingness to keep momentum moving forward? The opposite is being completely brainwashed by that one-track influence, which will dictate how you view the decision and all the actions that are born from it. Literally, your every fibre of your being will be influenced, from how you socially engage with others and how you talk or bitch about the decision, how you treat others because of the decision, and right down to how you view yourself and your belief in your self-worth and ability. To put it simply, to give power to those loud opinions we manifest can result in us becoming jaded and resentful, on a self-sabotaging and debilitating level.

This is a self-empowering approach I have always adopted from as early as I can remember. Some of my earliest memories are associated with fitness and training. I would say to myself the little affirmation, 'The more I'm hurting, the more fun I'm having'. I wore it as a badge of pride all over my face, that in the depths of a challenging workout, no matter what the intensity of agony or discomfort I was feeling inside, I would do my best to be projecting a calm, composed, calculated, and almost disconnect face to those around me. For me, this was one of the greatest feelings of fulfilment, and one of the most potent fuels to the fire stoking and forging the armour of my character and resilience. Knowing, that no matter how much my mind, and body disapproved of what it was feeling, sometimes that's an understatement, but is screaming to stop, that not only was quitting or throwing in the towel the furthest thought from my mind, but that I was able to remain consciously aware and in control of how much of that pain I was projecting to the world. This is not a statement of ego, for me it was always deeply internal, reinforcing to me that I can encounter the greatest challenges and adversities in my life, both physically and mentally, and know that I will always have the composure and clarity to embrace them with integrity and a humbled resolution of resilience that I know has limitless stamina. The person who goes knocking on the door of the devil will always get an answer; it's the person who can look the devil in the eye and smile who is their own master. Don't allow that ego too much time on the microphone. Take it back and remind yourself of your deepest inner truth.

Chapter Seventeen

"Overcoming my own adversities."

Since writing this and reliving and reflecting on many of the situations I encountered, or interactions I had, I've been amazed at how clearly your thoughts and feelings can come back to you when you intentionally try to recreate that moment. Every detail, sight, sound, sometimes smells and even thoughts and feelings in the then present are brought back to life, like they've been branded in your psyche. My time with SAPOL has been one of the greatest roller coasters of my life, experiencing the full gravity of highs and lows throughout my time. I only say has been, because I never presume that the best is behind me, or I'll never attain such amazing heights. I'm a big believer in realising your own greatness and knowing, without seeing that there's more you're destined to experience and haven't even felt in your life yet. For a long time before SAPOL, that destiny I fantasised about was serving in the police. It was a dream in my mind that carried the same weight of someone wanting to arrive in Hollywood and get their big break. So many times, I would have a moment of pause and just allow the true scale of the dream, the need to fulfil it wash over me. Late nights sitting in Flinders University library, working on an assignment, and I've got my headphones in, my bangers playing, and that one song comes on that elicits that fantasy and the clarity of your dream and the clear intention of it comes to the forefront of my mind. In these moments, I'd stop what I was doing and allow the sudden wave of elation wash over me, feeling my chest rise, my heart flutter, tension in my fist and a physical pulse that was like a charge finding its way out the top of my head. Despite all the odds, and the only certainty I could hold onto being that the successful outcome was far from guaranteed, those sweeping moments of elation and appreciation were powerful driving forces, like a sonic wave travelling through you and suddenly reminding you of how much this ambition meant to me.

Once I was in, actually living the dream I'd had for so long, I would periodically remind myself of these moments. Especially during challenging times, I would reflect on those moments of daydreaming and how much I was willing this dream to be realised, and that would bring a degree of thankfulness into the present, so I could be grateful for this opportunity I was now living. This was a powerful strategy, and many times it kept my feet grounded, and allowed me to focus on what was within my immediate control so I could persevere through the challenge ahead of me, regardless of the result, but with clarity that I knew I would move forward without compromising myself, and ultimately seeking my own fulfilment and resolve along the way.

One of the earliest examples of this was back in the Academy. It was a Saturday morning, and I was doing the 11:00 a.m. class at Street Defensive Tactics, where I trained in Krav Maga/Self-Defence. We were doing warm-up drills, that mimicked close-quarter strikes. In this case, standing close to your partner face-to-face and with little to no room to punch or kick, using the inside of your forearm like a sledgehammer and striking them to their upper arm (this was simulating an armbar strike to the side of the neck, which a strike that heavy with that much force to the carotid artery of the neck, is pretty much an instant knockout). Because it was such a close and sudden strike, I wanted to emphasis the torque from my hips to produce instant explosive power with no wind-up. I threw my right hip forward and allowed my right arm to follow like a relaxed whip the moment before tension. On impact, I felt a sharp and deep pain, like someone pouring hot water under my skin, flow through my right pectoral muscle (my chest muscle) without pausing I threw the left side with the same intention and velocity, and the same intensity of pain shot through my left pec. I slightly staggered but didn't let on to my partner or anyone that anything was wrong. As the class continued and the coach was speaking to us, I could feel myself in mild shock, I felt like the blood from my head was drained and I felt nauseas and queasy. As we were doing a grappling drill, I was with the coach and despite pushing through and hiding from showing him anything was wrong, I realised certain movements with my arms caused a sudden cramping like pain through my chest, and the strength and control in them was almost non-existent.

I booked in to see a physiotherapist at the earliest opportunity to assess the damage. I had a minor tear, low-grade in both pecs. While the reality of the situation was looming over me, I didn't actually feel any distress or panic over the very real prospect of what might happen that being, if I was physically injured for long enough during my time at the Academy and missed enough training or scenario assessments due to this incapacity, then I might be back-coursed. That's being removed from your course and placed in another course a few weeks, or months behind you, so you can cover the material again and gain competency. This was the pressure cooker environment in the Academy. Struggle enough times or fail to show competency, then you could very well be pushed back by a few weeks and be mixing with an entirely different course.

I remember going into the classroom on that Monday morning. By this time, I had black and purple bruising covering half of my pecs, and up the inside of both my arms. I can't really remember, but I think our first class for the day was OST, with the physical training instructors. This meant, we started the day in our training attire, dark blue T-shirt, blue shorts, and a blue baseball cap. I remember because at the start of the day when everyone was talking about their weekend, I told one of my mates what happened and showed him the bruising. I still remember his face. At the class, I picked my moment to approach one of the instructors and confess what had happened. From the first time I saw him, I'd nicknamed him the Blonde Terminator. The first time he came into our classroom, probably in our first week, with our head OST instructor to introduce themselves, he made an impression. While the head instructor introduced himself and explained all about the OST program, this guy stood with a stoic, stern look on his face looking over us. When asked by the other instructor if he wanted to add anything to the group, he replied with enough to reassure us of what was coming, "Nah."

I approached him and he maintained his tough exterior, but I remember his persona softening in the slightest when he saw my bruises and realised the nature behind me approaching him. For the next few weeks, I was on the side-lines for OST sessions, which for a person who loves anything fitness, and physical, this got old pretty fast. The prospect of back-coursing never entered my mind, and if it tried to, I was quick to dismiss it and reassure myself that it would never happen, and I would do whatever it took to avoid it. I would reassure the instructors by giving them updates each time I saw the physiotherapist, giving them an indication of my recovery and when I would be back to full capacity. At about this time, I spoke to our OST head instructor. As it turns out, I had known him from years earlier, when we'd been members at the same CrossFit gym. Whether this played any part in me avoiding being back-coursed, I never knew for sure, or as he had said to me, my physical abilities and performance were never a concern, and I had previous training in self-defence, which some of the assessments revolved around approved restraint techniques. When I was approved for full duties again, one lunch time, he took me into the training room, and for a few minutes, I demonstrated some of the necessary drills. He never let on if he was cutting me a break, and he was an exceptional and fair trainer and I would have expected no special treatment regardless of our history, but I was just thankful that he was patient with me and my recovery and gave me the opportunity to put his mind at ease and allow me to progress on.

Despite the usual stumbles when you're at the beginning stages of a new career and applying all new skills in an otherwise foreign and unknown environment, a lot of the adversities I began to encounter were self-imposed and playing throughout my head. When I was on the road, if I was given feedback, or criticism, I would take it on and perhaps overwhelm myself with it. For example, when at Hindley Street, after a while the speed of my paperwork and computer prowess was raised. I became very quiet and internal in the typing room, pretty much a large office full of computers for any officer to complete their investigations and paperwork. I would try to avoid the usual banter and chatter that went along in there and put my focus and attention into what I was working on. Perhaps in this way, I was at times seen to be too serious or involved in it, and maybe some perceived it as withdrawn, but as I was learning, particularly when some of my performance was scrutinised, I would often take to great lengths to improve it.

Overtime, my own self-inflicted adversities started to feel like walking on eggshells around some. I think I became to a degree, self-conscious of my performance and both not wanting to make a mistake (at least in the eyes of my seniors) while not inhibiting the potential I believed I had inside. I began to see that elements of my personality perhaps weren't a natural fit within the police, and the thrills and elation I had always imagined from serving in uniform were becoming faded. I am a thriving person around positive energy, openness, and connectivity with others. It's a fact, in policing you're exposed regularly to the worst in people, forever staring into the dark abyss of human nature, mental health, degradation and poverty. I would find myself arriving at crossroads, questioning what impact this constant exposure would have on my own desire to connect and how I still saw the world and other people. Because some of the practices in policing were not coming naturally too me, this caused my own doubts to question if this really was the career of a lifetime for me.

Funnily enough, and an ability I was always proud of whenever it was required or tested was my willingness to go hands on with offenders. As I had found out on Hindley Street, of all the instinctive subconscious psychological reactions we have when we are faced with danger or a threat, fight, flight, and freeze, fight was my automatic response, or at least, the instinct to run towards the threat. Chasing suspects on foot, restraining them on the ground, running into the middle of an altercation, these all came natural too me. I didn't perceive threat or fear, I simply had enough belief and commitment within myself to run through a wall if I needed too or run through fire to get to someone. For the record, I never did either of those things.

The who of it never affected me either, whether it was a big burly aggressive guy or an emotionally distressed hysterical adolescent girl. When it came time to respond, I knew that was automatic in me.

Towards the end of my career, as I was still on a Plap. To see some of my performance criteria rise, SAPOL wanted to do whatever they could to support me and assist me in my development. I had no influence or say in making an appointment with a SAPOL Psychologist, just like the decision to move from Hindley Street to Holden Hill was not mine to make. So, I had a couple of these pre-arranged appointments, SAPOL's way of checking off if there were any psychological reasons for me not progressing or if they could identify if there was anything they had missed that they could utilise to support me and put a new strategy in place. One of the psychologists had been in SAPOL over 30 years. She had been a detective sergeant (or a similar high rank) in Major Crimes or CIB and was now an inhouse support. We spoke for a couple of hours, and it was a relief to share honestly and openly the personal conflicts and doubts I had been experiencing but resisting for some time. She quickly ticked all the boxes and could see there was nothing for SAPOL to be concerned with, but that, as she put it, I was a square peg trying to fit in a round hole, and my personality perhaps wasn't a good mesh within SAPOL. A lot of what she said was very accurate and I could only agree with her on many things, which gave me reassurance regarding things I'd been thinking or feeling. At the end of our chat, she simply said, "Nic, you're a fascinating person." Or something along those lines. She made a curious observation; she pointed out how most officers that she spoke too didn't want to be there. They were feeling overwhelmed with pressure, their minds were in an unhealthy and unstable place. She said they would be sitting there clammy, tense, and avoiding eye contact with her at all costs. But she said with me, I appeared relaxed, even enjoying the conversation we were having and the fact that I was even there having to speak with her. It got me thinking, and I was quite open in sharing that this was a welcomed opportunity to speak openly and honestly with someone and engage in an immersive and explorative conversation. While it was not my call to arrange an appointment, I respected SAPOL for trying whatever they could to support me and saw no reason not to feel comfortable. Actually, months before this appointment, this casual outlook on the underlying reasons for SAPOL arranging these sessions did get me into some trouble.

I remember on this particular night; I had gone to Muay Thai training. I might have even been on nightshift later that night, but this is all based on vague recollection, some of it is clear, some a bit blurry. I was in my car after training, and I got a phone call. It was the senior sergeant from Hindley Street Station. He was checking in with me and chasing me up as I had been a no-show at a booked time with a SAPOL psychologist. In my own underestimation, I did not appreciate the red flags that not showing up for an appointment like this raised throughout different areas. I knew I was mentally solid, and well aware of some of the pressures and struggles I was managing, but felt they were well within my mental fortitude, so when the time came to attend the appointment, whether I had prioritised other activities, I disregarded any urgency to attend. By doing this, alerts had been sent from the SAPOL Psychological Sector to my team, my brevet sergeant and my sergeant and had even gone through them to the managing officer of Hindley Station, the senior sergeant. Once he could obviously tell that I was not suffering any mental anguish, and that it was simply a case of my not appreciating the seriousness and necessity of the appointment, we spoke briefly on a more casual basis, and he offered plenty of positive reinforcement for my support and progress moving forward. I'm pretty sure that the next time I was on shift, my brevet sergeant had a few things to say to me too.

As I discuss some of these different types of adversities I was encountering, I should mention that through realising these conflicts, I was able to take somewhat of an impartial step back in my own mind, like a third party witnessing the conflict for themselves, but remaining grounded, non-judgemental and calculated in the perspective they formed about why this conflict was happening, and what did it mean? That's the power of being able to subdue your own ego and look within yourself without judgement and think about the very thoughts you're having in a patient and inquisitive way. By doing this, I became comfortable with the feelings of unsettlement and conflict within me towards certain things. I enabled myself not to look at them with a defeatist mind or opinion of myself, but rather to try to understand what parts of me these conflicts were battling with. I sought reasons within myself that I was proud of and gave intentional effort to accepting that these were qualities of mine that are strengths, but perhaps they're not able to be fully expressed or utilised in this environment. Perhaps this dream that I wanted for so long, and was so grateful to be living, is not meant to be my destiny, but rather an invaluable experience to help me discover much more about myself and where my traits can be of much greater service.

Chapter Eighteen

"Crossing over a thin blue line."

In the weeks leading up to my resignation, small glimpses of realisation were settling in, and I was paying very close attention to them. I was still somewhat wrestling with my conscience over this prospect, and I wanted to be absolutely clear, with no doubt in my mind and no prospect of regret in the time after I leave, that this was not something I wanted to hold on too.

Right up until the end, some aspects of the role still felt unnatural too me. After being a police officer for nearly two years now, I felt that after this much time, if I'm not feeling natural in the role, and feeling like so much of the experience is something I'm still trying to force, rather than flow and embrace, perhaps that's a feeling that's trying to tell me something. Call it a gut instinct, but if we feel a looming certainty about ourselves within a particular environment, if it goes on long enough, we can be doing ourselves the greatest disservice by ignoring it. There's pride and accomplishment in still pushing through, being strong willed, maybe even stubborn and refusing to backdown, even within ourselves. But this instinct had been swelling in my gut for a long time, and once I had embraced the inevitable prospect of moving on, turning the page, and finishing this chapter in my life, there was an instant wave of relief that came over me. I was no longer trying to cling to something, gritting my teeth and forcing myself to hold on, but I had accepted the free fall, the freedom of letting go and trusting within myself that I was only going to fall forward into the next calling in my life. Even if in this immediate moment, I didn't have complete clarity into what that was.

One strategy I had employed within myself, to still persevere through this and will myself to succeed, was asking my sergeant to let me go out solo, out on patrol on my own. Admittedly, I was still a probationary, which this period had been extended out numerous times to support my performance development. Yet after nearly two years, I felt confident in ways I could do things, and handle myself. I was confident, and perhaps I didn't project this enough to my peers, in our protocols, investigations and processes. I generally felt like I could take a fleet out on my own and respond to almost any tasking and have the knowledge and capability to walk into it, make decisions and solve problems and enforce the appropriate legislations. I had thought of it before, I realised I knew a lot more than I even gave myself credit for. If I had been patrolling solo and happened to see a suspect trying to mug a person, I had the instinctive knowing to communicate my call sign, my location, description of the suspect, direction they were heading, and that I would be attending to the victim, if they needed paramedics and grabbing the necessary information from them. That's if the suspect saw me and bolted. If I caught them by surprise, I would restrain them with all the force in my muscle fibres, and then communicate via radio to comms all the above, plus that I had one suspect restrained, under arrest and I was safe on scene. I genuinely believed I had that capability and know-how with where I was in my probation. Sometimes, I feel like I held myself back based on the perception I felt my seniors and colleagues had of me, and their faith in my competency. My respect towards the hierarchy meant I didn't challenge at times where I trusted my outlook on the situation. They had their self-assurance forged after years and years of being in the role, so rather than stepping up enough and saying I've got this, I want to take this one, I resigned myself to their experience and natural instinct to take charge. So many times in my mind, given the potential risks and consequences that were always present in what we did, I did what I felt best served the greater good, and would ultimately see a successful outcome, and working alongside someone with more experience and more knowledge in that situation seemed to me to be the best road to follow to achieve the best outcome. Perhaps I wasn't willing to make enough mistakes, knowing there could be serious consequences, even to other people, but at the same time, I knew I had the courage to jump in no matter what was happening. Fear was never an inhibiting factor for me. I came to realise it was not backing myself enough to take the lead, not trusting enough in what I knew I could do in front of my colleague. This was a reason why I felt going out solo sometimes might help me break through that psychological barrier, as I would have no one to rely on except myself, and I would be forced to take chances and solely trust in my own abilities, rather than being able to fall back on an experienced colleague.

Although, I did have one moment where I threw all that behind me and took a chance by responding to a tasking solo. We were on day shifts, which meant we finished up, without any last-minute incidents, back at base at about 3:00 p.m., to drop equipment so arvo (afternoon shift) could be kitted up and ready for patrols. I was with a patrol partner that day, but for whatever reason they had already gone inside. A call came over the radio that a male was seen at a nearby KFC, in the garden with what looked like a firearm. From memory, the details were something similar that came over the radio, because something in my mind decided that I was already in a position to get there as quickly as possible. Arvo shift were not kitted up yet, and technically, we were still on shift. It was not uncommon that incidents could occur within minutes of you dropping your kit and being done for the day. In these situations, if the tasking was urgent and could not wait for the next shift, you would get there as quickly as possible, but you knew the sergeant for the next shift was already delegating patrols who would be hot on your tail and would relieve you and take over the job. Working overtime was not a common occurrence, and SAPOL never encouraged it. In fact, if you knew you would be doing even an hour of overtime, that had to be approved in the moment by a much senior member, such as an inspector (or someone around this ranking).

But anyway, I digress again. I can remember the seriousness of the report that came over the radio, and instinctively I responded back that I would attend. It was just around the corner from the station. I jumped back in our fleet and took off for the location. I began playing through my actions and requirements once I got there if I happened to locate a male with a firearm. My phone was already ringing from my sergeant, concerned about what I was doing. I think deep down I knew this decision would be, in one way viewed as wrong as I am a probationary and should be in company with a partner and not running solo to a potentially high-risk situation. At the same time, I had clear justification in my mind why I had chosen to do this. I wasn't out to prove to anyone, and I responded to the possibility of fewer innocent lives being lost if I was in a position to get to the location faster than anyone else (as the other shift were in the middle of distributing equipment). Even further down, I feel like I was proving something too myself, that I could step up and do this job. Perhaps I had been grilled for something earlier or knowing there were some things in my probation performance that were not viewed as up too standard, this was my way of brushing the eggshells aside, and running straight through them with a clear sense of resolve and trust in my ability and why I had to do this. Even in the face of criticism, I took a risk.

I got to the location and drove around for a while, trying to sight a dodgy looking character in the bushes, lurking around anywhere or if people were running in all directions from somewhere. In my mind, I was at the absolute ready to hold up the road, draw my firearm and go head-to-head with a male holding a rifle the second I sighted him, like a wide-eyed lion staring down a gazelle the second before it charges. Don't take that to sound egotistical, but that's what the intensity, focus and readiness felt like when you were on the hunt for a suspect that you knew had every potential to become violent; your mind and body was ready for combat. I couldn't see anyone or any signs that there was any cause for concern or any disturbance at all, so I made my way back.

I didn't receive any grilling for making that decision, in fact, perhaps senior members would feel a sense of relief when they know a probationary has the gut instincts to run towards danger in the heat of the moment or jump into the fight when all hell breaks loose. I was proud I had backed myself and responded, at the time it was all about preserving life. But I recognised there was an element of risk in me stampeding into that job alone. What if I had confronted a person with a firearm? Alone or not, my responsibility and duty as a police officer was all empowering, and in that uniform, I could have stood face to face with an Army if I knew it was necessary to uphold the law and protect innocence. So many times, my fight response was dictated by the fearless and selfless commitment to the oath we had taken when being sworn in way back on our day of Graduation from the Academy. What I found when acting on my own instincts, was how all the training and experience I had accumulated, suddenly kicked in, it became my shield and sword. I felt like a vessel, fuelled only by calculated and tactical thoughts, readying myself for multiple scenarios I envisioned so I would respond in the necessary way, once confronted with the situation. It was an electrifying feeling, and one I would experience countless times throughout my career.

Chapter Nineteen

"The greatest thing that will never happen to me."

The title of this chapter I took from a quote I heard from the Rock, Dwayne Johnson. He said it when he was describing his ambitions and dreams as a young man to play in the NFL. But he was suddenly cut, and that dream was shattered. Well, for the Rock, the rest is history. He became a superstar legend in the WWE and has gone on to be one of the biggest blockbuster superstars in Hollywood and business tycoons walking the planet. To him, playing in the NFL, realising that dream is the greatest thing that never happened to him, because that sudden change in trajectory set him on a path of even greater accomplishment and stardom. Since leaving the police, that has resonated in my mind a lot. I had dreamt of serving in the police for so long, for years. Finally getting my opportunity on my third application. After walking into the Academy, first day thinking I was about to commence my career for life, and living that dream for nearly three years, I came to realise that it would be the greatest thing that will never happen for me. I had to experience it to realise for myself that that wasn't where I belonged, that's not what my true calling in life was, that I had something else in me to express, and that wouldn't be fulfilled as a police officer. I realised this quickly in my career but dismissed those unnatural blockages and resistance in myself as merely skills and experience that I hadn't yet grown into. Yet after nearly two years of working as a police officer, so much still felt unnatural too me, and I couldn't ignore a gut instinct telling me that I wasn't meant for this long-term. No matter how much I had tried to convince myself otherwise. For this, and so many other reasons, the countless experiences I had, the amazing, courageous, selfless and heroic people I served alongside and who mentored and invested so much into supporting me, the growth and depth of self-discovery I went through, these are just some of the reasons why the dream of becoming a police officer, of serving through my entire working life is why this is the greatest thing that will never happen for me. I spent years dreaming about it, a short time living it, but I'll be forever grateful for experiencing it.

Unbeknown to me at the time, my experience in the South Australia Police was revealing the true trajectory of my life's purpose. My untold story and the true calling I was destined to answer. Helping me to recalibrate my aim, and bit by bit, like a mentor with a comforting hand on my shoulder, turning me to face clearly, the path I should be following. What I discovered, only months after leaving SAPOL, was I had never even considered what I would do, or who I would be after police. As I talked about earlier, receiving that phone call in Perth, realising my dream had actually come true, and that I would be making a living doing something I had dreamt about for so long, that moment felt like I had reached the top of my mountain. My career, and everything it would create for me in the future was sorted. I would actually be earning a salary, in the career of my dreams. Knowing that's not a claim everyone can enjoy, I felt truly elated and deeply grateful. Then as my career got underway, and small doubts or questions began to reveal themselves too me. Conflicts within myself that I eventually couldn't ignore, and some of these conflicts inhibiting my own ability to perform to set expectations. I say conflicts meaning internal struggles about my place in this world, if this service was where I was truly going to discover a deepening sense of fulfilment, or if the nature of it was going to cause me to disconnect from certain passions that I just couldn't exercise in the police. I resisted for so long, convincing myself what I was capable of, and often repeating to myself how much this meant too me, reminding myself of all those times I would sit in the car, close my eyes, and imagine myself actually being a police officer. I tried to remind myself of that elation and that now I was actually living it, so be relentless and persevere to succeed. Eventually, I accepted I was not destined to always be in this uniform, but that transition out didn't fully sink in until months after leaving. But what I would eventually discover, would be where my natural abilities and strengths would be of the greatest service, and I can only be grateful for the abundance of unique and confronting experiences, and discovery of self in SAPOL to help me realise where and how I can have the greatest impact.

Chapter Twenty

"Reflections and realisations."

There's not a day that goes by now, where I don't think of my time in the police. I am easily reminded of it anywhere I go. Sometimes that's locations I happen to be in or drive past where the memory of an incident I was in there is suddenly triggered. Hindley Street is now a place I have no reason to visit, or even pass through in transit. I may catch up with a friend near it for a coffee or a drink, or on the very rare occasion, even end up back down it on a night out. I can't even remember the last time I was there for anything. Reflections and realisations like that I find fascinating, because for about ten months of my life, I spent majority of my days and nights patrolling the street of dreams and its surrounding area. For that time, I lived only a twenty-minute walk away, with a mate in a townhouse. So, Hindley Street and the city was my life for that chapter. Now it's a distant echo, and I'm only in the city to visit my gym. Every once in a while, when I drive past Hindley, I'll take a peek down it, where all the memories, arrests, brawls, foot chases, patrols, interactions, and time spent with my teams come flooding back to me in a chaotic whirlwind of snapshots, like an album of memories caught in the wind. Even when I'm training at my gym, I could be doing the 6:15 p.m. class and be reminded when I would do that same class time, but I was working nightshift. So, get a workout in, and start work at 11:00 p.m. The same feelings of anticipation and readiness come back to me. I am always very proud and deeply grateful anytime I pass a police vehicle pulled over on the side of the road and see the officer interacting with the driver. Some of my instincts and connection to SAPOL are always there, and I find myself keeping a close eye on the officer, and the situation knowing that if I ever saw one in a physical confrontation or any bad situation, instinctively I would stop my car in the middle of the road and sprint over there in a heartbeat to help them. I'd like to think any good standing, decent person with integrity would do the same thing if they saw a police officer in trouble, to the best of their ability of course. When you have served in uniform, and you've been in that same position as that officer, knowing how ever present the risk is, and how in an instant, a seemingly calm and casual interaction can turn into anarchy, and knowing just how very real and dangerous the risks can be, your instincts are idling anytime you see a police officer with someone. They wouldn't have to know me, but having both worn that uniform, and had the courage and character to uphold what it represents, that's always worth protecting and fighting for. In my mind, that's a bond, similar to what military would experience, that is internal forever.

It's 12 minutes after midnight as I'm writing this and realising that I'm nearing the end of writing something that has been a consistent project of mine for over a year. Pouring my heart and soul out to simply share my story and have a tangible reflection of one of the most surreal chapters in my life. I think it's important to finish with some of the most important lessons and realisations I took away from what was easily the most challenging and most honourable three years of my life.

Never quit chasing a dream. Should the day ever arrive that that dream is realised, the gravity in that moment is one of the strongest feelings of euphoria you can ever experience, and you'll realise in everything and anything else you do, that that feeling is what you want to chase every day. It doesn't have to happen today, or even tomorrow, or in a few months or even a few years away. But that feeling of obtaining and accomplishing something you've wholeheartedly invested yourself in, fantasised about in a moment of daydreaming, and believed that there is some possibility against insurmountable odds, that you can have it; a life spent in pursuit of that feeling alone, is a life fulfilled.

Believe in yourself, beyond the expectations you assume in your own mind, that others have towards you. This was a valuable, somewhat confronting realisation I had throughout my time on probation. So often, I would find myself questioning my own course of action, or I could see the outcome necessary, and I could see the actions in front of me to take to achieve it, but in my inexperience, I would follow the example of my experienced senior colleague with a sense of comfort that we were serving the greater good, and that outcome would be the best one possible. I was humble and gracious enough to put myself aside, yet I feel this was a detriment because it could be perceived as inability or lack of competence. As hard working and reliable as my attitude could be, looking back perhaps I didn't trust in my gut enough and challenge or step up, regardless if there were mistakes made along the way. There is never anything I do in my life that is at random or not thoughtfully considered and justified in some way, and even if I could see there was a difference of opinion in the eyes of a colleague, no doubt from faith they've acquired over years of trial and experience, too often I would not take hold of my own decisiveness and instinct, and respectfully follow the path of my senior. Some of this was born through what I perceived in my own mind, was their opinion of my capability, which would make me question my own ability, and hesitate in the face of making a mistake, rather than standing my own ground and backing myself through the difference of opinion of others. Basically, this lesson I realised is not putting superiority of another on your shoulders. There's being gracious and respectful in the face of a senior member and showing that respect towards their confidence and experience. However, courage is found in trusting your own intelligence, decisions and abilities and owning the opportunity to express them. Even against experience and self-assurance, people are unique from one another, and where your own understanding and knowledge of something may be far reaching, another's may not extend as far. Their lack of willingness to sponsor your way, can simply come from a lack of knowledge and understanding, coupled by the fact that how they've done something has always worked for them. This is not to say their way is right, and your way is wrong, it simply means that when you both observe the same situation, your ways of solving it will vary, just as your personalities are not the same, but one is not superior or inferior to the other. I had amazing mentorship during my time in uniform, and as my experience and confidence grew, I think at times I still suppressed myself, based on the façade of the scenarios and perceptions I had manufactured in my own mind. Risk believing in yourself, because in the end if your actions and motives come under question, without having completely shit the bed of course, perhaps your reasoning can educate others on something they just didn't know yet.

Fear is an illusion. There is nothing scarier in this world than our own ways of seeing it. Coming face to face with fear, or what many might perceive as fear inducing was a common occurrence on duty. The sudden call to a major high-risk job, that sends your senses, adrenaline and anticipation into rapid overdrive. Making your way to an incident knowing you're entering a volatile and violent situation, or about to confront a dangerous person, a psychotic person, mass hysteria or a graphic and traumatic scene. I came to realise that fear and apprehension stemmed only from our own uncertainty and self-imposed doubts as to how we could function in such a situation. The fear was never external, but rather ignited internally from external factors. If a person becomes violent, aggressive, threatening, they appear like a morbid frenzied distorted beast intent of standing over you and even hurting you, if you see them for exactly this, you can feel three feet tall and completely powerless. However, having the humbled assurance in yourself that you have the capabilities to confront that force, and the courage and willingness to do whatever you can, beyond all comprehension of others fear is replaced with focus and intent. Fear is a fear of the outcome or a consequence. That angry frightening person is scaring me because they might physically hurt and injure me. I am up really high up, if I fall, I could die and never see my loved ones again. If I don't get over 80% on this exam, I could fail this course, which could stop me graduating and then what happens to my career? Like in scary movies, the fear is induced from the anticipation and what you cannot see. My understanding of it at least, is fear is born from uncertainty from within. Preparation, presence, and patience in the moment can all dissolve fear and enable in your mind a sense of clarity and assurance as to what you have to do. Overcome the fear of uncertainty and the possibility of what hasn't occurred, and you'll be in the present state of now.

Self-awareness, self-reflection, and a constant desire to question your satisfaction in any moment, and seek the answers are the foundations of momentum and self-discovery. So much in policing, I was either hyper aware in the present moment, or reflecting on what just happened. This was triggered by the countless situations I found myself in. Whether it was something extreme and intense, or my own feelings towards what was required of me, and how fulfilled and satisfied I would be over a long-term. I was constantly self-analysing and actively seeking another means or solution and trying to apply it to better my circumstances. For example, in the later part of my service, when some of my performance standards were under question, and I was feeling both these and self-imposed pressures. On my way to shift, I would reflect on criticism I had received, and I would rehearse in my mind how I could show I was applying that feedback. I might say to myself, today I will step up and tell my senior member I am taking the lead on every job we have. I would ask myself questions, and answer them with deliberate action-inducing words or phrases, such as "How do I want to interact with my colleagues? I want to be engaging, positive, and enthusiastic. How do I want to feel the moment I walk through the door of the station? I want to feel self-assured, reactive, and ready for anything, confident in what I can do. Or how do I want to project the moment I walk into that situation? With assertiveness, take-charge and take control." With self-awareness, I was able to recognise how I was feeling in any given moment, I could strategize how best I could show up in the next moment, and I could constructively receive feedback and utilise it for my own progress, rather than it debilitating me. Self-reflection and seeking answers to my own questions gave me a sense of comfort and assurance, that I was motivated to raise myself, my own standards and performance. It was reassurance that I was existing each day caring about myself and the effort I applied. Without this accountability we have no momentum day to day, and a few things are inevitable. We will never know what it feels like to exert ourselves, to be confronted with our own limitations and actively strive for our potential. We will never fully grasp how much something means to us, and how we can live everyday with purpose, drive, and intention.

Sometimes, the thing you think you want the most, or something you are willing to attach your life purpose and identity too, won't turn out to be your life. Before SAPOL, I could clearly envision policing as more than a career too me. It would be my calling in life, I would identify myself as a police officer, and I would be willing to make huge sacrifices to live up to that. But something I had not really anticipated, was what if this wasn't the fairy tale for the rest of my life? What if this wasn't the chosen path for me? As I progressed in my career, the reality slowly set in that I would no longer be a police officer, something I had dreamt of and aspired too for years. But with acceptance of that, eventually that opened a freeing sensation of excitement and possibilities. I had realised my dream, I had committed to it, worked hard for it, and was given the opportunity to live it. All I could reflect on from that entire experience was the gratitude I had for it. I have never looked back on it as any kind of failure, but only a necessary chapter that inspired in me new depths of self-awareness and discovery. I feel like this could ring true with anyone who looks back on a specific chapter in their life. Looking back with regrets, failures, resentment or even hatred are only inhibiting your own sense of self-exploration and expression. Even a person or experience that was the cause for so much horror in your life, if you can look hard enough, you can be grateful for the strength, resilience, and self-belief it forged in you. Carrying around those past unresolved opinions, are like dragging a tonne of boulders, when you're still trying to walk forward. Having a sense to reflect back on them with a degree of acceptance, and even appreciation and gratitude, for the awareness, strength, and ability you have today, is like walking forward freely, but taking the time to stop, look back, and appreciate that pile of boulders you've left behind.

My service in the South Australia Police has been and will always be one of my greatest achievements and honours in life. From the day I printed the application and filled in my name at the top, the day I finished the final stage of selection, receiving my phone call of acceptance, my first day walking into the Academy and the day I marched out, countless memories serving in Hindley Street and Holden Hill, to the day I walked out of Holden Hill station for the very last time having returned all my police equipment; there's not a moment that I am truly grateful to have lived in and experienced. So many of them fuel me today, to chase and work towards those moments in our life, where we feel, sometimes in that very brief but ultra-present place in time, the exhilaration and overwhelming sense of accomplishment, pride, and realisation.

I began writing this autobiography simply to have a record of my own thoughts and feelings, realising that so much of what I had experienced was interesting, or even unbelievable. I got to walk in the shoes of a police officer, an occupation that so many dream of, from a very young age and so many will try for but never get to experience. It was as close a feeling at times as I could get to feeling like a superhero, functioning in situations, doing things, interacting with people that even in the moment, there was still a sense of is this really happening? I've realised this book is a raw account of my time entering and immersing in a world that's truly unbelievable, challenging at times beyond understanding, and more rewarding and fulfilling than you can ever prepare yourself for. As I reflected on my time in uniform, and recorded everything, I wanted it to be a no-holds-barred account of my thoughts, feelings and reflections. Even more truthful at times as I would accept to myself, as so much of it highlights traits of me that were destined to never be suited to the life of a police officer. It's as raw to me to read over as when those confronting thoughts and realisations first came into my mind. But it's equally a celebration for who and how I showed up every day to serve. When I decided that one day, I would love for others to read my story, I wanted the accounts of what happened, to be coupled with my honest and open reflections and perspective. If one person takes the time to read this cover to cover, I will be deeply humbled, because I believe there are some valuable life lessons, affirmations, realisations, and inspirations that could touch a person at a moment in their life that shines a light on their current circumstances, or helps them realise more about themselves, or gives them courage to take the first step along a new pathway. We all have a legacy to leave in this world, and this story will be a big part of mine.

As I started this, I can only finish by holding my hand to my heart, closing my eyes, and whispering a deeply resounding thank you, to every officer I was privileged to work alongside. From my mentors and instructors at the Academy, who personified the courage, principles, and values that a police officer lives by, and inspired in us as new, young, and eager cadets. Thank you to my course mates from the Academy, and any other cadet I shared a conversation or a smile with. Hopefully, this sees you still serving to the full capacity of your potential and testament to you for committing to a truly fulfilling and lifechanging career. Thank you to every member from every team I served on and alongside. Even a short time in your presence, left a lasting impression on me, and I aspired to only strive harder to represent the courage and dedication you showed me. Thank you to every one of my field tutors during my probation. There was such a mixed bag of personalities amongst you, styles, and strategies you all brought as my senior partners, but I never lost sight of the most inspiring trait that connected all of you. You were my mentors, my teachers, and you all were unwavering in the dedication, support, encouragement, stamina and commitment you showed me every day in investing in my development and progress. Often times I didn't voice my gratitude enough, but I know that was never sought after, and in your minds that degree of selflessness and commitment is simply a natural part of who you are…you are heroes, you are police officers, and even though it is simply coming from me, you were all an inspiration every day.

The only thing necessary for evil to conquer is for good people to do nothing.

I served with good people who did something. I served with police officers. I served with heroes.

www.ingramcontent.com/pod-product-compliance
Lightning Source LLC
Chambersburg PA
CBHW060510290526
45791CB00001B/341